A Miscellany for Dancers

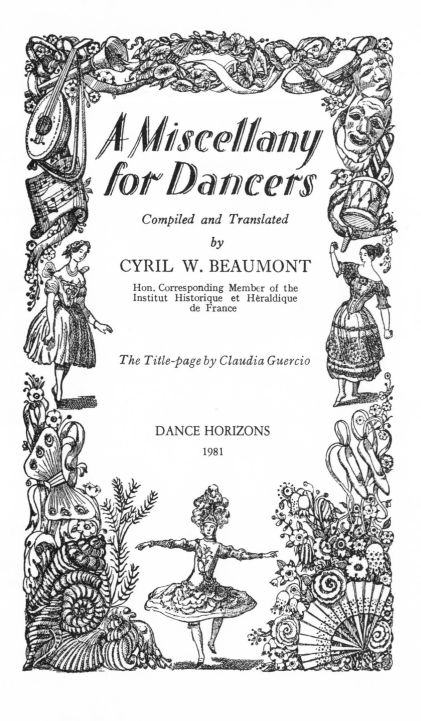

A Miscellany for Dancers

Compiled and Translated

by

CYRIL W. BEAUMONT

Hon. Corresponding Member of the
Institut Historique et Héraldique
de France

The Title-page by Claudia Guercio

DANCE HORIZONS

1981

TO

MY WIFE

ISBN 0-87127-122-2

Library of Congress Catalog Card Number 80-69957
Printed in the United States of America

Dance Horizons, 1801 East 26th Street, Brooklyn, N.Y. 11229

1 2 3 4 5 6 7 8 9 10

PREFACE

This anthology is intended to afford a glimpse of well-known dancers from the eighteenth century to the present day, both on the stage and off, and at the same time to present a composite picture of the life of a dancer from the period of training to the farewell performance. The extracts, with the exception of Chapter III, are confined to exponents of the art of classical ballet.

All the quotations from works by French authors have been translated by me, unless stated to the contrary, and in this connection I am indebted to my old friend, Mr. de V. Payen-Payne, for many valuable suggestions.

I also wish to record my indebtedness to Dr. Pierre Tugal, the erudite Keeper of *Les Archives Internationales de la Danse*, Paris, and his staff, for having kindly traced for me the sources of the Balzac and Baudelaire quotations cited on pages 12 and 16 respectively.

The Grisi letter quoted on page 103, and all those contained in Chaper XI, with the exception of the Taglioni letter dated 24th November, 1835, are in the collection of M. Camille de Rhynal, President of the *Syndicat National des Professeurs de Danse et Danseurs Professionnels*, Paris, who courteously permitted me to copy the originals and reproduce them in an English rendering.

I am indebted to Miss Melusine Wood for permitting me to quote from the translation of *De Practica seu arte tripudii*, by William the Jew, which was made for her by Signora A. Maccheroni.

I have to thank the management of the Savoy Hotel, London, for information respecting the two dishes described on pages 189 and 190.

Last, but not least, I am greatly obliged to the following authors and publishers for permission to quote from the works here named—MM. Bloud et

Gay (Paris) : *La Danse au Théâtre* by André Levinson. Messrs. The British-Continental Press : *The Story of the Russian School*, by Nicholas Legat. Messrs. The Clarendon Press : *Works*, by Lucian, translated by H. W. Fowler and F. G. Fowler ; *The Oxford English Dictionary*. Mr. Anton Dolin and Messrs. Sampson Low, Marston & Co., Ltd. : *Divertissement*, by A. Dolin. MM. Duchartre et Van Buggenhoudt : *La Danse d'Aujourd'hui*, by André Levinson. Mme. Thamar Karsavina and Messrs. William Heinemann, Ltd. : *Theatre Street*, by T. Karsavina. Mme. V. Nijinsky and Messrs. Victor Gollancz, Ltd. : *Nijinsky*, by Romola Nijinsky.

C. W. B.

CONTENTS

I

DANCING DEFINED

Dancing is silent poetry.

Simonides.

*

Dancing is an action showing outwardly the spiritual movements which must agree with those measured and perfect concords of harmony which, through our hearing and with earthly joy, descend into our intellect, there to produce sweet movements which, being thus imprisoned, as it were, in defiance of nature, endeavour to escape and reveal themselves through movement. Which movement of this sweetness and melody, shown outwardly (when we dance) with our person, proves itself to be united and in accord with the singing and with that harmony which proceeds from the sweet and harmonious song or from the measured sound we are listening to.

William the Jew, of Pesaro,
de Practica seu arte tripudii.

*

Dancing, so to speak, is to jump, to hop, to prance, to sway, to tread, to tip-toe, and to move the feet, hands and body in certain rhythms, measures and movements consisting of jumps, bendings of the body, straddlings, limpings, bendings of the knees, risings on tip-toe, throwings-forward of the feet, changes and other movements.

Thoinot Arbeau. *Orchésographie.*

*

Dancing is an elegant, and regular movement, harmonically composed of beautiful attitudes, and contrasted graceful postures of the body, and parts thereof.

John Weaver. *Anatomical and Mechanical Lectures on Dancing.*

*

Dancing is no more than knowing how to bend and straighten the knees at the proper time.

P. Rameau. *Le Maître à Danser.*

*

Ordered movements of the body, leaps, and measured steps made to the accompaniment of musical instruments or the voice.

Diderot and D'Alembert. *Encyclopédie.*

*

Dancing is an art because it is subject to rules.

Voltaire. *Siècle de Louis XIV.*

*

Dancing is a manner of being.

Honoré de Balzac. *La Paix du Ménage.*

*

Dancing consists of nothing more than the art of displaying beautiful shapes in graceful positions and to develop from them lines agreeable to the eye ; it is mute rhythm, music that is seen.

Théophile Gautier. *Histoire de l'Art Dramatique en France depuis Vingt-Cinq Ans.*

*

Dancing is the expression of pleasure or other sentiment by means of prescribed movement, regulated by music, either imagined or expressed.

Friedrich Albert Zorn. *Grammatik der Tanzkunst.*

*

Dancing is the pure act of metamorphosis.

Paul Valéry. *L'Ame et la Danse.*

*

Dancing is the continuous movement of the body

travelling in a pre-determined space in accordance with a definite rhythm and a conscious mechanism.

André Levinson. *La Danse d'Aujourd'hui.*

*

A rhythmical skipping and stepping, with regular turnings and movements of the limbs and body, usually to the accompaniment of music.

Oxford English Dictionary.

II

IN PRAISE OF

DANCING

Socrates—that wisest of men, if we may accept the judgment of the Pythian oracle—not only approved of dancing, but made a careful study of it ; and, in his zeal for grace and elegance, for harmonious movement and carriage of the body, thought it no shame, reverend sage that he was, to rank this amongst the most important branches of learning.

Lucian. *Of Pantomime.* Trans. by
H. W. Fowler and F. G. Fowler.

*

Dancing or saltation is an art both pleasing and profitable which confers and preserves health, is adapted for the youthful, agreeable to the aged, and very suitable for all, so far as it is employed in fit place and season, without vicious abuse.

Thoinot Arbeau. *Orchésographie.*

*

The art of dancing has ever been acknowledged to be one of the most suitable and necessary arts for physical development and for affording the primary and most natural preparation for all bodily exercises, and, among others, those concerning the use of weapons, and consequently it is one of the most valuable and most useful arts for nobles and others who have the honour to enter our presence not only in time of war in our armies, but even in time of peace in our ballets.

Letters Patent, 1661, *for the establishment at Paris of an Académie Royale de Danse.*

All the ills of mankind, all the tragic misfortunes that fill the history books, all political blunders, all the failures of great commanders, have arisen merely from lack of skill in dancing. . . . When a man has been guilty of a mistake, either in ordering his own affairs, or in directing those of the State, or in commanding an army, do we not always say : So and so has made a false step in this affair ? . . . And can making a false step derive from anything but lack of skill in dancing ?

Molière. *Le Bourgeois Gentilhomme.*

*

Dancing being that which gives graceful motions all the life, and, above all things, manliness, and a becoming confidence to young children, I think cannot be learned too early. . . . Nothing appears to me to give children so much confidence and behaviour, and so to raise them to the conversation of those above their years, as dancing.

John Locke.
Some Thoughts concerning Education.

*

So much of dancing, at least, as belongs to the behaviour and a handsome carriage of the body, is extremely useful, if not absolutely necessary.

Eustace Budgell. *The Spectator*, May 17th, 1711.

*

Dancing adds graces to the gifts which Nature has bestowed upon us, by regulating the movements of the body and setting it in its proper positions. And, if it do not completely eradicate the defects with which we are born, it mitigates or conceals them. This single instance will suffice to explain its utility and to excite a desire to be skilled in it.

P. Rameau. *Le Maître à Danser.*

*

Dancing's a touchstone that true beauty tries,
Nor suffers charms that nature's hand denies.

Soame Jenyns. *The Art of Dancing.*

You must dance well, in order to sit, stand, and walk well, and you must do all these well in order to please. . . . Take particular care that the motions of your hands and arms be easy and graceful ; for the genteelness of a man consists more in them than in anything else, especially in his dancing.

Lord Chesterfield. *Letters to his Son.*

*

Dancing is the veneer to education.

Jean Etienne Despréaux. *L'Art de la Danse.*

*

Dancing can reveal all the mystery that music conceals.

Charles Baudelaire.
Fanfarlo des Paradis Artificiels.

*

Life would probably have far more meaning and light if, side by side with the teaching of reading and writing, people were also taught to dance beautifully.

Anna Pavlova.
Quoted Victor Dandré. *Anna Pavlova.*

III

OF DANCING-MASTERS

HOW TO RECEIVE A DANCING-MASTER

The student should meet the master on his arrival and receive him with fitting courtesy, then make him two bows, the first very low, the second less so ; he should then show him into the room and invite him to be seated in an arm-chair or chair. As soon as the master (lady or gentleman) is seated, the pupil will hold out both his hands, place himself in the first position and make four bows (the knees well turned out), the first very low, the second less so, likewise the other two, taking care not to raise his heels.

The bows accomplished, the pupil will walk forwards, then backwards, to the right or left, and in any other manner that the master may deem fit.

The lesson at an end, the pupil will have the courtesy to attend the master to the door of the room ; he will then make him two bows, the first low, the second less so, and politely thank him for all the trouble that he has taken.

Guillemin.
Chorégraphie ou l'Art d'écrire la Danse.

A DANCING-MASTER AT HIS STUDIES

I was awakened this morning by a sudden shake of the house ; and as soon as I had got a little out of my consternation, I felt another, which was followed by two or three repetitions of the same convulsion. I got up as fast as possible, girt on my rapier, and snatched up my hat, when my landlady came up to me, and told me that the gentlewoman of the next house begged me to step thither, for that a lodger she had taken in was mad ; and she desired my advice, as indeed everybody in the whole lane does upon important occasions. I am not like some artists, saucy because I can be beneficial, but went immediately. Our neighbour told us, she had the day before let the second floor to a very genteel man, who told her he kept extraordinarily good hours, and was generally at home most part of the morning and evening at study ; but that this morning he had for an hour together made this extravagant noise which we then heard. I went upstairs with my hand upon the hilt of my rapier, and approached the new lodger's door.

I looked in at the key-hole, and there I saw a well-made man look with great attention on a book, and on a sudden jump into the air so high, that his head almost touched the ceiling. He came down safe on his right foot, and again flew up, alighting on his left ; then looked again at his book, and holding out his right leg, put it into such a quivering motion, that I thought he would have shaked it off. He used the left after the same manner, when on a sudden, to my great surprise, he stooped himself incredibly low, and turned gently on his toes. After this circular motion, he continued bent in that humble posture for some time, looking on his book. After this, he recovered himself with a sudden spring, and flew round the room in all the violence and disorder imaginable, until he made a full pause for want of breath.

In this interim, my women asked what I thought. I whispered that I thought this learned person an enthusiast who possibly had his first education in the peripatetic way, which was a sect of philosophers who always studied when walking. But observing him much out of breath, I thought it the best time to master him, if he were disordered, and knocked at his door. I was surprised to find him open it, and say with great civility and good mien that he hoped he had not disturbed me. I believed him in a lucid interval, and desired he would please to let me see his book. He did so, smiling. I could not make anything of it, and therefore asked him in what language it was writ. He said it was one he studied with great application ; but it was his profession to teach it, and he could not communicate his knowledge without a consideration. I answered that I hoped he would hereafter keep his thoughts to himself, for his meditations this morning had cost me three coffee-dishes, and a clean pipe.

He seemed concerned at that, and told me he was a dancing-master, and had been reading a dance or two before he went out, which had been written by one who taught at an academy in France. He observed me at a stand, and went on to inform me, that now articulate motions, as well as sounds, were expressed by proper characters ; and that there is nothing so common as to communicate a dance by a letter. I besought him hereafter to meditate in a ground-room, for that otherwise it would be impossible for any artist of any other kind to live near him ; and that I was sure several of his thoughts this morning would have shaken my spectacles off my nose, had I been myself at study.

I then took leave of this virtuoso, and returned to my chamber, meditating on the various occupations of rational creatures.

Addison, *The Tatler*, No. 88, November 1, 1709.

GAETANO VESTRIS GIVES A LESSON IN DEPORTMENT
TO THE PRINCE DE LAMARCK.

" Now then, Prince, are you ready ? Bow first— bow— Her Majesty the Empress of Germany—Ah ! Lower sir, lower (*very quickly*) ! You will wait three-quarters of a second before rising—good.

" As you rise, sir, you must turn your head quietly and modestly towards the right hand of Her Imperial and Apostolic Majesty. Kiss that hand which sways the sceptre (always without daring to raise your eyes to look upon the august face of that sovereign).

" Your features, sir, are to be quite expressionless while you make your bow to so great a princess ; a demeanour implying respect and even awe is essential and not inappropriate at a moment so fraught with consequences for physical grace.

" You will imagine, if need be, so many dazzling crowns, so many superb titles, supremacies, altitudes, centuries gone by, combats to the death, and other grandeurs, that you will naturally become quite overwhelmed.   That is the whole of the matter.

" Now, Prince, bow to the Landgravine of Hesse-Darmstadt !   Ah, that is too low !   Too low by four inches !   You bow to her as though she were a Queen—have a sense of proportion, sir, proportion ! And now once more—so, good, *bravissimamente !* But, although you are only bowing to a Landgravine, you must remember that she descends from the Imperial Court of Luxembourg !

" Look at the venerable lady-in-waiting and say, with a smiling air : ' If it were not for etiquette, Madame la Comtesse, I should grant you all the homage which I owe to your kindness, your virtues, your great age, and the position which you hold at Court.'

" Now, sir, I should like to see how you would bow to the wife of the Constable of Rome.   Oh !   Prince, how you—how you pain me !   Is this the outcome of all my experience, care, labour, and zeal ?—That will not do, Prince—it is too low for you, too low ! God forgive me, but you take an Excellency for a Royal Highness and make her a humble bow as though you were a countrified nobleman !   Let your manner imply : ' Princess, my heart is gladdened that my visit to Rome has made it possible for me to salute so illustrious a lady, the beauty of beauties, who honours her country by patronising the fine arts.' Then go back quickly to the side of the Prince of Palestrina, the Constable's eldest son, whom you will find in his mother's *salon*, because he has been notified of your arrival at the Colonna Palace.   Alas,

alas, *sango di mi !* What do I see ? Am I bereft of my wits ? Dear, dear—my poor young man ! You bow with that solemn English style which is only suitable for bestowing alms on convicts. There, see him well rewarded for his kind intentions ! And what happens, Prince ? He looks coldly at you, he picks you to pieces, criticises you, hates you—he is your enemy ; no matter nothing can be done to alter it.

"Remember this, sir, for a future occasion, and when you see his brother, Don Gaetano Colonna, let your pleasing manner seem to say before you speak : ' I am really charmed to make your acquaintance ; I desire your friendship and offer you mine (this with a proud and able manner), it is worth having.'

"Without wishing to weary you with injunctions, let me advise you, Prince, that you will find the demeanour I have suggested much the most successful. Believe me, that foolish, stiff-necked air of *qui s'y frotte, s'y pique*[1]—Charlemagne's motto, I think, but it does not matter—will never withstand a winning manner.

"Now, sir, let us descend a few degrees ; let me see how you would bow to a famous artist. Be generous. Take care what you are about and do not hurry ! See in a celebrated artist the happiness of a vast empire, a person of naught who climbs to the stars, a man whom monarchs cherish, ennoble, and enrich ! Imagine you see the aged Vestris, honoured with a pension, wearing a black ribbon[2] (which I should be wearing now, but for that hellish Revolution) ! Imagine I am the Chevalier Vestris ! Bow, sir—bow—a little lower ! "

Marquise de Créquy. *Souvenirs.*

[1] Whoever meddles with it, will rue it—the same meaning as the motto of the Order of the Thistle : *Nemo me impune lacessit.*

[2] Allusion to the French Order of Saint Michael (founded in 1469 by Louis XI), the badge of which was worn attached to a ribbon of black watered silk. The order was abolished on the outbreak of the French Revolution, but temporarily revived during the Restoration.

MONSIEUR ABRAHAM THE DANCING-MASTER

The dancing-master, M. Abraham, radiated an extreme gravity. Imbued with the importance of his art and his sacred memories of the French Court before the Revolution, proud of having taught French graces to that beautiful Marie Antoinette of whom he obligingly quoted several Austrian awkwardnesses during his first lessons ; prouder still of being the only one to preserve to the present day the great national traditions of the Menuet, with the correct interpretation and graduated *pliés* of the *révérence*, M. Abraham held himself in high honour. He never visited the houses of his noble pupils except in a carriage and attired in full dress. He entered and departed, sat down and rose, spoke, scolded, coughed and blew his nose, always in the most ceremonious manner. The fingers that he rested on the bow of his kit were covered with enormous diamonds, each of which, so he said, had been given to him by some Queen or Princess Royal. From his hoary wig to the gilt buckles on his dancing-shoes, from his fine lace *jabot* to the black silk stockings drawn tightly over his false calves, everything in him aimed at majesty of demeanour. M. Abraham carried his years lightly because of his supple limbs, which rose and fell in cadence. His steps, when he executed them before parents—he never took this trouble for a mere pupil—displayed a consummate precision and youthful ease. Even his breathing was ageless and seemed like the rest of his person, to be subject to that lofty decorum of which he constituted himself the representative.

Daniel Stern. *Mes Souvenirs* (1806-1833).

A PUPIL WHO BROUGHT NO HONOUR TO HIS MASTER

Whilst a resident at Paris, being duly intent upon a little improvement in matters of personal grace, he [Lord Sandwich] had recourse to a *maître de danse*, whom he described to have been a very civil and obliging person, and of whom, when quitting

Paris, he inquired if he could serve him in London, to which the grateful Frenchman, making his best bow, replied that " he had only to entreat of his lordship never to tell any one of whom he learned to dance."

G. Yates. *The Ball ; or, A Glance at Almack's in* 1829.

MARCEL REBUKES HIS PUPIL

A lady who had been a pupil of this distinguished professor [M. Marcel], and remained subsequently his steady and zealous friend, succeeded in obtaining for him from the government a pension for life. In her great joy at having such a boon to put into his possession, she advanced to him—the certificate in her hand—with a hurried and anxious step ; when M. Marcel, shocked at the style of presentation, struck the paper out of her hand, demanding if she had forgotten his instruction ? The lady immediately picked it up, and presented it with due form and grace ; on which the accomplished Marcel, the enthusiastic professor of his art, respectfully kissed her hand, and with a profound bow exclaimed : " Now I know my own pupil ! "

G. Yates. *The Ball, or ; A Glance at Almack's in* 1829.

DESPRÉAUX GIVES A LESSON FIRST TO MARIE LOUISE AND THEN TO NAPOLEON

The day after the marriage, Napoleon went to Compiègne, and, the day following, he sent word to me to give the Empress lessons in deportment. So I betook myself to Compiègne, where I arrived a little late, owing to the difficulty of procuring post-horses. As soon as I arrived at the castle, I was warmly welcomed. Duroc gave me a room in the palace. Two hours later, some important persons arrived and I was asked to give up my apartment, receiving in exchange another at the other end of the castle. I dressed and went to wait on Her Majesty the Empress, but she was with the Emperor. When I returned to undress, I was told that my room was wanted for an ambassador who had just come. So, after this, I made up my mind to go and put up in the town. . . .

Here is an account of my first meeting with the Empress.

I had been told to come at eleven in the morning. I went to the castle where I was ushered into a circular drawing-room. I waited and rose at every sound, expecting to see Her Majesty enter ; but it was only chambermaids who came to look for a ribbon or something, although I believe they only came in out of curiosity.

Then a person dressed quietly in white came in, her head held low and her arms hanging down at her sides. I rose at once and made her a low bow. . . . I then drew on my gloves, took her hand, and began my lesson by making the Empress walk. The Queen of Naples entered just when I was engaged in a little argument with Her Majesty who, when stepping forwards, was most careful to put her foot down toe first. The Queen of Naples adroitly broke off the lesson, took me aside, and said I was right ; such a manner of walking was illogical, and that Abraham, her old dancing-master, had taught her the reverse, likewise her children.

I then said to the Empress : " I humbly beg Your Majesty's pardon, but I cannot permit such a fault to pass. Because, if, in stepping forwards, the foot is to be placed on the ground toe first, then, in stepping backwards, the heel should come first."

Hardly had I uttered these words than the Emperor entered. " Good day, M. Despréaux," said he, " I see that you are very busy." Then, turning towards Marie Louise, he remarked : " Madam, be sure you do everything that M. Despréaux bids you, because I shall not take you to Paris until you are able to walk, to hold yourself correctly, and to dance."

I then spoke to Napoleon. " Your Majesty, her deportment cannot be altered as soon as one would like—it is the same with all habits. Her Majesty has acquired the habit of walking with her head down and her stomach out." " Well then, Madam," interrupted the Emperor, " you must push your —— out backwards."

I dare not repeat the word used by Napoleon. The Queen of Naples, a lady-in-waiting, and Mme. Murat were there, and not one dared to utter a word. They were petrified with astonishment at this language of the gutter.

I immediately took the Empress by the hand and made her walk as majestically as possible, guiding her with whispered instructions. Having raised my voice a little to bid her lift her head up and keep her chin from resting on her chest, the Emperor said very loudly : " Yes, yes, you are right. You used to bear yourself like an Arch-Duchess, now you must bear yourself like an Empress."

I instantly saw from these words that the Emperor realised the gravity of her fault. He walked proudly towards a large mirror and made a number of low bows, saying each time : " Well, M. Despréaux, is that right ? "

" Your Majesty," I replied, " respect is shown in the quickness with which one sinks to the ground and in the slowness with which one rises, rather than in the largeness of the movement. The bow of an inferior consists in sinking quickly and rising slowly. Contrariwise, the bow of a superior consists in sinking slowly and rising quickly." Napoleon approved of my observations and bade me teach him to waltz.

He placed his arm on my shoulder and we prepared to begin ; but, as soon as I felt that the pressure he exerted would bring us both to the ground, I begged him to stop. He at once ran to Marie Louise, gave her some little taps on the cheek, kissed her, and wished her to dance with him.

But there was no violinist because, thinking the lessons would be restricted to deportment, I had not thought to bring one with me. The Emperor rang and commanded a violin in the castle to be brought. They brought one, but no one could play it. Then Napoleon said to me: " But you, Despréaux, who do so many things, doubtless you can play the violin."

So I took the instrument and, with plumed hat under my arm and sword at my side, I played the violin and danced with the Emperor, who leaped like a goat, telling me that he had learned differently with a celebrated professor. For over half an hour he bounded well in time with the music but keeping his knees bent.

He then spoke of the dance called *Les Tricotets* and when I mentioned that it was Henri Quatre's favourite dance, he wanted to dance it at once, although he knew none of the steps ; so, still holding my three-cornered hat under my arm, my sword at my side, and my violin in my hand, I faced Napoleon and tried to teach him the steps of the *Tricotets*, while His Majesty, perspiring, tried to copy me and execute the steps beloved of Henri Quatre. Napoleon found the dance charming and I had the unfortunate idea to suggest that at the next court ball he might have a quadrille devoted to this dance, with the dancers dressed in costumes of the period. He replied : " Yes," but his expression said : " No."

I had thought I was still at Versailles and it had not occurred to me that Henri Quatre would not go well with the new court.

> Jean Etienne Despréaux. *Souvenirs.*

A DANCING-MASTER OF THE EIGHTEEN-FORTIES

The   dancing-master's   physiognomy,   at   the

Académie Royale de Musique, is rather a curious one. When a dancer after thirty years of loyal services, has lost his elasticity, and cannot any longer spring from the ground—when he is tired, worn out, foundered, he becomes a professor. The dancing-school is to him what Greenwich Hospital is to disabled sailors. He writes on his cards: "Polydore Larchet, late first dancer at the Académie Royale de Musique, dancing-master at the Académie Royale de Musique."

Polydore Larchet is a little man who walks with his head upright, his foot bent, and his arms gracefully bowed. He wears a fair wig, a light-blue dress coat, yellow inexpressibles quite tight, and thin shoes at all seasons. He is a faithful adherent to the classical style of dancing, and makes, but with reluctance, some concessions to new methods. He will, on all occasions, remind you that he has had the honour of dancing at Erfurth before Their Majesties the Emperors Alexander and Napoleon, and that the great ladies of the day were delighted with his personation of the river Scamander. He takes off his hat when the name of Vestris is pronounced in his presence and maintains that Louis XIV was the greatest king we ever had, because he was the most elegant dancer of his time.

But you should see M. Polydore Larchet in his school: his cold dignity is admirable; he never gets impatient, and always uses the most select expressions. When he addresses his pupils, even the youngest, he invariably employs the most polite forms. "Mlle. Julia, will you be so good as to turn out your toes. Mlle. Amanda, do have the kindness to raise a little more your left arm." Polydore is the last representative of French gallantry.

Jules Janin and others. *Pictures of the French.*
The above extract is taken from *The Pupil of the Academy*, by L. Conailhac.

A DANCING-MASTER'S EPITAPH

(Taken from a tomb at Llanbeblig, Carnarvonshire)

Here Lie the Remains of
Thomas Chambers
Dancing-Master
Whose genteel address & assiduity
in Teaching
recommended him to all that had the
pleasure of his acquaintance
He died June 13, 1765
Aged 31

IV

THE MAKING OF A DANCER

THE TRAINING OF MARIE TAGLIONI

As a professor of dancing, M. Taglioni showed himself as exacting, as unbending to his pupils as M. Duprez, in his character of professor of singing ; they made of their daughters, the one a great dancer, the other a fine singer. Abundant sweatings, overwhelming fatigues, tears, nothing moved the heart of this father, dreaming of the glory attendant on the talent that bore his name.

Dr. L. Véron. *Mémoires d'un Bourgeois de Paris.*

*

I have seen Mlle. Taglioni, after her father had given her a two-hour lesson, almost drop dead on the carpet of the room, when she let herself be undressed, sponged, and re-dressed, without seeming to know what was taking place. The agility and marvellous bounds seen at the evening performance were purchased at this price.

Albéric Second. *Petits Mystères de l'Opéra.*

TWO FAMOUS TEACHERS AND TWO SCHOOLS OF THOUGHT

Like the artists of great epochs of painting, M. Taglioni established a new school of dancing, very different from the style and philosophical thought of the Gardels and the Vestris. These two schools offered even a piquant contrast. Vestris taught grace and seduction, he was a sensualist. He demanded provocative smiles, poses and attitudes verging on the indecent and shameless. I have often heard him say to his pupils in a cynical voice : " My dears, be charming, be coquettish ; display the most captivating freedom in all your movements ; you must, both during and after your *pas*, inspire passion. . . ." The school, style, and language of M. Taglioni expounded the exact opposite, he demanded a graceful ease in the execution of every movement, airiness and particularly elevation, *ballon* ; but he allowed no girl to employ a gesture or pose lacking in decency and modesty. He used to say to his pupils : " Ladies, married and unmarried, should be able to see you dance without having occasion to blush ; take heed therefore that your dancing be distinguished by austerity, delicacy, and good taste.

Dr. L. Véron. *Mémoires d'un Bourgeois de Paris.*

HOW A DANCER WAS TRAINED IN THE EIGHTEEN-FORTIES

I was barely seven years old when I was sent . . . to M. Barrez's class, at 4 Rue Richer. I went out in the morning with my stomach empty, except for a cup of what was said to be coffee. I had neither shoes on my feet nor a shawl on my shoulders, and, as often as not, my thin muslin dress was threadbare like lace. I arrived shivering and famished. Then the daily torture began, a torture of which my description, however exact it may be, can afford only the feeblest impression. Banished from the legal code, torture has taken refuge in dancing-classes.

Each morning the master imprisoned my feet in a grooved box. There, heel to heel, and knees turned outwards, my martyred feet became accustomed to remain in a parallel line. It is called " turning oneself out " (*se tourner*).

After half an hour of the box, I had to undergo another form of torture.

This time, it consisted in placing my foot on a bar which I held with the opposite hand to the foot being exercised. It is called " stretching oneself " (*se casser*).

These labours accomplished, you doubtless think that I revelled in a rest. Good gracious, does a dancer ever rest? We were poor wandering Jewesses to whom M. Barrez ceaselessly cried: " Dance! Dance! " After we were " turned out " and " stretched," we must, under pain of the master's displeasure, or even his slaps, study *fouettés*, *assemblés*, *jetés*, *balancés*, *ronds de jambe*, *cabrioles*, *sauts de basque*, *pas de bourrée*, and, lastly, *entrechats quatre*, *entrechats six*, and *entrechats huit*.

Such, sir, are the pleasing elements which constitute the art of dancing. And do not imagine that such hard labours last but a short while. They must always endure and be ceaselessly renewed. On such terms only can the dancer preserve her suppleness and lightness. A week of rest must be paid for by two months of redoubled work without respite. The dancer is the personification of Sisyphus and his rock.

Albéric Second. *Petits Mystères de l'Opéra.*

COSTUMES WORN IN CLASS IN THE EIGHTEEN-FORTIES

The costumes worn by *danseurs* and *danseuses* in class resemble those worn by Paul and Virginie, as I have seen them represented at the Ambigu Comique by M. Albert and Mlle. Eugénie Prosper. The women are bare-headed and low-necked ; they have bare arms, their figures are imprisoned in tight bodices. A skirt, very short, very puffed out, whether in gauze or striped muslin, reaches to the knee. Their thighs are chastely hidden beneath large calico knickers, as impenetrable as a state secret. The men, without ties and bare-necked, are dressed in little coats of white dimity and short breeches reaching half-way down the leg, secured at the waist with a leather belt. It is almost like the stage ; but do not ignore the fact that there is a great gulf between the adverbs *almost* and *quite*. In fact, it is the stage minus the illusion of limelight and perspective, minus the seductions of wet-white and the falsehoods of vegetable red. I have no hesitation in asserting that a dancer at class is not at all captivating or poetic.

Albéric Second. *Petits Mystères de l'Opéra.*

CORALLI TAKES A CLASS

" Saulnier," said old Coralli, " that pose is worthless—do it again."

And Saulnier repeated the pose.

" But have I not already told you that you represent Pleasure ? " the choregrapher went on. "Where the devil have you seen Pleasure frowning, pursing her lips, and poking her head forward like an ox chewing the cud ? Do the pose again."

New effort on the part of Saulnier ; further failure ; another movement of rage from M. Coralli.

" Oh, the hussy ! Oh, the slut ! A weapon ! Give me a weapon, somebody, so that I can rid the Opéra of this disgrace ! "

And since he had no weapon in his hand, he pulled off his hat, seized his wig, and, with a strong arm, flung it full in the poor dancer's face.

The irritable Frederick having arrived, M. de Coislin was not long in appearing on the horizon. Two minutes later, M. Coralli was kneeling before his victim, beseeching her pardon and replacing his wig.

Albéric Second. *Petits Mystères de l'Opéra.*

*

M. Coralli, the ingenious choregrapher to whom you are indebted for *Giselle* and *La Péri*, gives lessons at all prices. His class is very large. M. Coralli is at once the most courteous of men and the most irascible of ballet-masters. He is Frederick, King of Prussia, understudied by M. de Coislin. Oh, prodigy of will power ! It has succeeded in combining these two natures, although so distinct and so opposed. Gracious me, how fine he looks, when, in the midst of his class, having given an order which his pupils carry out badly, he cries in a resounding voice :

" A thousand million thunders and devils; curse it, what a set of fools you are ! That is to say, no —ladies, will you be so very kind as to take the trouble to carry out a little of what I told you. I should be most grateful to you. If not, I shall kick you all out ! "

Albéric Second. *Petits Mystères de l'Opéra.*

AN UNUSUAL METHOD OF " TURNING OUT "

Mlle. Nathalie [Fitzjames] thought out a new method of " turning herself out " (*se tourner*) and " stretching herself " (*se casser*) at the same time. She would lie down on the floor, with her face to the boards, and her legs stretched out horizontally. Then she made her servant stand on her and press down with all her force on that portion of the anatomy where, as that joker D'Arnal used to say, the back changes its name.

Albéric Second. *Petits Mystères de l'Opéra.*

THAMAR KARSAVINA HAS A LESSON FROM HER FATHER

Father [Platon Karsavin] was a most exacting teacher, and when he sat there, his ever-present glass of tea by his side, he even assumed some sternness of manner. He never considered I had done my best unless sweat trickled down my face. He told me that when he worked for his *début* he literally sweated blood. He played a great variety of tunes for my exercises, bits of ballet music, bits of *Faust* and *Lucia of Lammermoor*, occasionally singing the words. His favourite was a Jewish polka. The one for which I often asked was the *Marseillaise*. The *grand battement* was not half so exhausting when done to its brave tune. Sharp, pithy remarks : " Do not hold your arms like candelabras ; knees bent like an old horse," urged me on. The occasional swish with the fiddle-stick I half resented. Father belonged to the old school of masters who believed that, unless a rigorous discipline is established, the pupil will let himself go. He taught me to put the utmost effort into every task. He got up occasionally to show me some steps. Once, feeling hot and thirsty, I took a gulp of tea behind his back. He checked me severely. " You will ruin your respiration if you do that," he said to me. Nor did he allow me to sit down directly after my lesson, explaining that a sudden relaxation of muscles after a great strain weakens the knees. Once changed, I had to walk up and down for some time like a race-horse before I might either sit or drink.

Thamar Karsavina. *Theatre Street.*

THAMAR KARSAVINA HAS A LESSON WITH CHRISTIAN JOHANNSEN

A Swede by birth, Johannsen spoke broken Russian intermingled with French. He had a vocabulary of oaths of uncommon wealth. " Pity you are weak-minded," he addressed me after each failure. " What a dancer I could have made of you but for that." He pointed to his forehead and then tapped the back of his fiddle. Epithets like " cow on the ice " rained on me. Once he was pleased with me, so much so that he called to Marius Petipa, who at that moment came in : " Come and see her *jetées en tournant.*" While I exhibited my *jetées en tournant*, Johannsen muttered sadly : " What a pity ! She could dance, but such a fool." Johannsen gave us very intricate steps, very difficult to fit to the music. He laid his fiddle across his knee and played pizzicato, using the bow only to point to someone faulty, nine times out of ten to me. " I see you. Don't you imagine I can't see your bumbling feet." A small tragedy happened once ; more than usually exasperated, he threw his fiddle-stick at me and called me " Idiot ! " On the point of bursting into sobs, I turned my back and left the room. Sergei followed me. " Come, angel, come and ask his pardon ; the old man loves you.

Be sensible." He led me up to Christian Petrovitch. I apologised. For the first time I saw him smile. " I taught your father," he said to me. He took my hand ; it was wet with perspiration. " Clammy," declared he, " your blood wants purifying. Drink Hamburg tea. Where have you been last night ? " " At a charity ball, Christian Petrovitch." " A ball indeed ! We never went to balls. That is why you stumble like an old crock. No balls for a dancer."

Thamar Karsavina. *Theatre Street.*

A LESSON WITH CATTERINA BERETTA

She was quite a dear, and such a funny creature. Once upon a time she had been famous for the strength and precision of her dancing. Now, she was a small, fat woman, and almost a pauper. She never rose from her arm-chair to show me a movement or a position. Always feeling cold, she wrapped herself in a shawl ; and often in the middle of a lesson would ask her old servant, Marcella, to rub her feet and cover them with a rug. . . . Signora Beretta was most imposing to look at. She usually carried a stick, with which she beat time, and when the lesson was over, we kissed her hand and she kissed our foreheads. Her big feet rested on a red velvet cushion, and she looked like an old queen.

Thamar Karsavina. *Souvenirs.*
(*Je sais tout*, Nov. 15th, 1912.)

A LESSON WITH MAESTRO CECCHETTI

We go up a flight of narrow, well-worn stairs ; then along the landing at the end of which is a door. We turn the handle and enter into a large, rectangular room. There is no furniture, save at the far end opposite the door. There, from right to left, is a piano, a fireplace, a large mirror, a revolving chair, another fireplace, a table on which stand vases filled with flowers, and, lastly, a comfortable settee. Along the three remaining walls runs a wooden bar. The walls are white with a black skirting. The room is lighted by four large windows covered for half their height with a glazed, transparent paper, patterned with roses and their leaves. On the walls hang innumerable pictures of Karsavina, Pavlova, Trefilova, Nijinsky and many others whose names are the history of the Russian ballet.

Presently Maestro Cecchetti enters with a rapid, impulsive step. He exchanges salutations with a quick nod of his head and twinkle of his eyes. He doffs his coat, seats himself in a chair, takes in his right hand a thin Malacca cane with a curved handle and prepares for the morning lesson.

From an adjacent dressing-room stream forth a number of girls and young women ; some in vari-coloured tunics, others in the conventional ballet skirt. In turn they exchange kisses on both cheeks with the maestro and the lesson begins with exercises at the bar, followed by centre practice and exercises on *port de bras*, *adage*, and *allégro*.

The relation between professor and pupils is that of a father and his children, but the maestro is none the less exacting. He conducts the lessons with the discipline and rigour of a drill-sergeant. Whistling an appropriate melody to each movement he emphasises the time with vigorous taps of his cane, which strikes the floor with the precision of a metronome. From time to time he rises from his seat to correct the curve of an arm, the position of a leg. His movements are expressive of his criticism. Skilful execution causes a faint smile to flicker over his lips ; he bows his head, which continually nods with pleasure. A careless movement and he springs upright with an angry shout, to let fly a boiling stream of mingled Italian and Russian words, the precise meaning of which it would be unwise to guess at. But, viewed purely as sound, Jove's thunders could not have been more terrifying.

C. W. Beaumont. *Enrico Cecchetti.*

V

PRECEPTS FOR DANCERS

THE ART OF DANCING

The art of dancing is not the knowledge of how to execute all manner of steps in accordance with a given rhythm—the latest recruit to the *corps de ballet* knows how to execute them ; quickness is but a feeble advantage.

A simple, correct manner of execution, consistent with grace—that is what is required ; to be able to leap high is a minor accomplishment. . . .

There are three kinds of grace : grace of form, grace of pose, grace of movement.

Grace of form is a gift of nature, it is rare. Grace of pose is the ability to select a position of the body consonant with good taste. Grace of movement is not merely the facility to pass from one pose to another, in accordance with the rhythm of the music, it demands expression according to the character portrayed, particularly in the dance *terre à terre*, which is quite different from the dance of elevation.

Despréaux. *Letter to Després*
(*Journal de Paris*, May 7, 1820).

*

To retain an airy grace in the midst of the most exhausting movements is the real problem in dancing, and such a virtuosity can only be acquired by the use of proper exercises suitable for the development of those qualities and for smoothing away the defects which everyone, even the greatest talents, has need to overcome.

Auguste Bournonville. *Etudes Chorégraphiques.*

PEARLS OF WISDOM

Let your body be, in general, erect and perpendicular on your legs, except in certain attitudes, and especially in *arabesques*, when it must lean forwards or backwards, according to the position you adopt. Keep it always equally poised upon your thighs. Throw your chest out and hold your waist in as much as you can. In your performance preserve continually a slight bend, and much firmness about your loins. Let your shoulders be low, your head high, and your countenance animated and expressive.

＊

Always draw your body well up, and especially your head, even in your minutest poses.

＊

In the performance of your steps let your body be quiet, firm, and unshaken, yet easy and pliant, according to the play of the legs and arms. But in this beware of stiffness.

＊

Take especial care to acquire perpendicularity and an exact equilibrium. In your performance be correct, and very precise ; in your steps, brilliant and light ; in every attitude, natural and elegant.

＊

A correct execution of an *adagio* is the *ne plus ultra* of our art ; and I look on it as the touch-stone of the dancer.

＊

Be vigorous, but avoid stiffness ; seek to acquire a facility of spring, that your *entrechats* may be easy, precise, and well crossed. Rapidity is also very pleasing in a dancer ; lightness, still more so ; the one imparts a brilliancy to his performance, the other has in it something of an aerial appearance that charms the eye of the spectator.

＊

Observe the *ballon* ; nothing can be more delightful than to see you bounding with graceful elasticity in your steps, scarcely touching the ground, and seeming at every movement on the point of flying into the air.

*

Ease and softness in the execution of your dance, I repeat, ought always to be aimed at. In this acquirement you show that the exercise is natural to you, and that you have overcome the greatest difficulty, namely, the concealment of art.

*

Never depart from true principles, nor cease to follow the best guides.

Carlo Blasis. *Code of Terpsichore.*

OF THE PRACTICE OF EXERCISES

In the *leçon* and exercises pay an equal regard to both legs, lest the execution of one surpass that of the other. I have seen many dance with one leg only; these I compare to painters that can draw figures but on one side.

*

Do not rely on your own natural qualities, and therefore neglect to study or practise so much as those to whom nature has been less liberal.

Carlo Blasis. *Code of Terpsichore.*

*

It is not so much upon the number of exercises, as the care with which they are done, that progress and skill depend.

Auguste Bournonville. *Études Chorégraphiques.*

*

Work not only till the sweat comes, but till the blood comes through the pores of the skin—only then you'll be a dancer.

Christian Johannsen. Quoted Nicholas Legat. *The Story of the Russian School.* Trans. from the Russian by Sir Paul Dukes.

OF THE DANCER

A dancer who wishes to charm the beholder's

eye must display all the elegance that his fancy can inspire him with, in the carriage of his body, the easy development of his limbs, and the gracefulness of every attitude into which he throws himself. But let no affectation intermingle with his dancing ; that would mar everything.

*

A good dancer ought always to serve for a model to the sculptor and painter.

Carlo Blasis.   *Code of Terpsichore.*

*

Un danseur quelquefois se borne à quelques pas ;
On a changé les airs, lui seul ne change pas.
Sans grace, sans maintien, il se présente en face ;
Il marche, il se promène, il court de place en place :
Là fait une attitude, ici des battemens ;
Il répète toujours les mêmes mouvemens.
Ses jambes, en dansant, ne sont jamais égales ;
La même fait toujours les ronds ou les ovales ;
Il fait vingt entrechats pour atteindre à la fin :
Excédé de fatigue, il disparaît enfin.
Fuyez de ces danseurs l'invention stérile ;
Variez, mais craignez tout détail inutile.
Tout ce qu'on fait de trop est fade et rebutant,
Et l'oeil rassasié se détourne à l'instant.
Sur les phrases de l'air phrasez aussi la Danse ;
Les momens de repos indiquent la cadence.
Ce pas était trop faible ; et vous le rendez dur :
Je veux être brillant ; et je deviens obscur :
L'un craignant de sauter, a trop de retenue :
L'autre a peur de ramper ; il se perd dans la nue.

Jean Étienne Despréaux.   *L'Art de la Danse.*

OF THE IMPORTANCE OF FORMING A STYLE

Of all the elements of his art, a dancer, like a writer, should make it his first business to cultivate a style ; and that style is more or less praiseworthy accordingly as it renders, expresses, and depicts elegantly the greatest number of exquisite, pleasing, and useful things.

If I were entrusted with the up-bringing of a young dancer in whom I perceived intelligence, some love for glory, and genuine ability, I should counsel him : " Begin by forming a style, but take care that it is suited to you. Be original if you aspire one day to make a name. Without this primary condition you can be sure of never achieving anything."

Cahusac. *La Danse Ancienne et Moderne.*

OF THE RELATION OF MOVEMENT TO MUSIC

Keep a vigilant ear to the movements, rests, and cadences of the music, that your dancing may be in exact concert with its accompaniment. Everything depends on this melodious union, and, when really perfect, it is charming in the extreme.

Carlo Blasis. *Code of Terpsichore.*

*

Le pas le plus brillant, la plus aimable danse,
Ne peuvent plaire aux yeux, s'ils blessent la cadence.

Des mouvemens confus n'offrent rien de brillant ;
Ils montrent peu de goût et jamais de talent.

Jean Etienne Despréaux. *L'Art de la Danse.*

OF TECHNIQUE

Master technique and then forget all about it and be natural.

Anna Pavlova.
Quoted Victor Dandré. *Anna Pavlova.*

OF EXPRESSION

Que la danse toujours, ou gaie ou serieuse,
Soit de nos sentimens l'image ingénieuse ;
Que tous ses mouvemens du cœur soient les échos,
Ses gestes un language, et ses pas des tableaux !

Delille.

*

Dancing, in common with all the arts, must say

something ; it must be expressive, it is a particular form of manifestation.

F. Lamennais. *De l'Art ct du Beau.*

*

A true artist should have no secrets. On the stage you must be able to transmit every emotion to the spectator.

Anna Pavlova.
Quoted Victor Dandré. *Anna Pavlova.*

OF THE DANCER'S ARMS

A dancer that holds and moves his arms in a graceful manner, according to the true rules of art, shows that he has studied at a good school, and his performance is invariably correct. Few artists distinguish themselves by a good style of action in their arms, which deficiency generally proceeds either from the mediocrity of principles they receive from bad instructors, or else it originates in their negligence, believing, as I have known many do, that if they possess a brilliant mode of execution in their legs, they can do very well without the fine additional ornament of the arms ; and thus exempt themselves from the labour which so important a study requires.

Carlo Blasis. *Code of Terpsichore.*

OF THE DANCER'S SMILE

She [Taglioni] notices, in looking at ballets, how often the dancers put on a smile and wear it, just as they put ornaments in their hair ; and she herself supposes some part of her marvellous power over the public to have lain in the fact that her smiles were never put on, but sprang spontaneously out of the joy which the delight of movement created within her.

M[abel] C[ross]. *Marie Taglioni.*
University Magazine, April, 1879).

*

A smile should hover about a dancer's lips like a

bird flutters about a rose, but it does not require to be fixed on those lips under penalty of mis-shaping them.

Théophile Gautier. *Histoire de l'Art Dramatique en France depuis Vingt-Cinq Ans.*

*

A dancer's prettiest smile began as a grimace.
Lemercier de Neuville. *Marie Petipa.*

THE COMPOSITION OF DANCES

Imitate a painter in your manner of combining and arranging ; let all the objects of your picture be in strict harmony one with another, the principal effect spirited, every tint (if the expression be allowed as relating to the modulations of steps, attitudes, etc.) flowing into each other, and the whole polished off with softness and taste.

Carlo Blasis. *Code of Terpsichore.*

*

Variety is one of the great charms of nature ; nor can you please the beholder for any length of time, but in changing often your compositions.

Dauberval. Quoted Carlo Blasis. *Op. cit.*

THE DANCER IN PRIVATE LIFE

In order to preserve unspoilt the pictures created by him, the artist should show himself to the public only on the stage, never in private life.

Anna Pavlova.
Quoted Victor Dandré. *Anna Pavlova.*

V I
DANCERS AS THEY STRUCK
THEIR CONTEMPORARIES

MARIE CAMARGO

Certain writers have erred in endowing her with graces. Nature had deprived her of everything she should have had ; she was neither pretty, nor tall, nor well formed ; but her dancing was vivacious, light, and full of gaiety and sparkle. *Jetés battus*, *royales*, and cleanly-cut *entrechats*—all these steps which to-day have been eliminated from the vocabulary of the dance, and which produce such a captivating effect, were executed by Mlle. Camargo with the utmost ease. She only danced to lively music, and such quick movements do not permit of the display of grace ; but for this she substituted ease, speed, and gaiety, and, in a piece where everything was depressing, long-drawn-out, and wearisome, it was a delight to see so animated a dancer, whose sprightliness could draw the audience from the torpor into which monotony had plunged it.

Mlle. Camargo was intelligent and she showed it by adopting a brisk style of dancing which allowed the spectators no time to detect and catalogue her physical defects. It is a fine thing to know how to conceal one's deficiencies beneath the lustre of one's talents.

J. G. Noverre. *Lettres sur la Danse, les Ballets et les Arts.*

MARIE SALLÉ

She was possessed of neither the brilliancy nor the technique common to dancing nowadays, but she replaced that showiness by simple and touching graces ; free from affectation, her features were refined, expressive, and intelligent. Her voluptuous dancing displayed both delicacy and lightness ; she did not stir the heart by leaps and bounds.

J. G. Noverre. *Lettres sur la Danse, les Ballets et les Arts.*

LOUIS DUPRÉ

A beautiful machine in perfect order, but lacking a soul. He was indebted to nature for the beautiful proportions of his physique, and the excellent construction of his limbs resulted naturally in smooth and flowing movements, and perfect harmony in the supple play of his joints. All these rare qualities gave him the air of a god. But he was always the same ; he never varied his style ; he was always Dupré.

J. G. Noverre. *Lettres sur la Danse, les Ballets et les Arts.*

JAVILLIERS

He took the place of Dupré, often with success ; and he had some special and some familiar steps which he executed gracefully and easily.

J. G. Noverre. *Lettres sur la Danse, les Ballets et les Arts.*

DUMOULIN

I have seen Dumoulin ; he danced the *pas de deux* in *La Bergerie Héroïque*, but I could only perceive in him the expiring gleams of a talent which, in its prime, might have been pleasing.

J. G. Noverre. *Lettres sur la Danse, les Ballets et les Arts.*

C. MALTER

I have seen Malter, nicknamed the Devil, because he took demon parts. He was vigorous, hardy, and spare ; always scared, he frightened nobody. This unreal and fantastic style has never been brought to

perfection. Our devils at the Opéra have nothing
in common with those of Aeschylus ; they are
well-behaved devils who would not even scare a
woman.

> J. G. Noverre. *Lettres sur la
> Danse, les Ballets et les Arts.*

L. MALTER

He was ever an indifferent dancer, but he trained
some pupils and was elevated to the dignity of
maître de ballet ; but as, at that time, a *maître
de ballet* lacked all inventiveness and never strayed
from the beaten track, Malter filled the post to
perfection.

> J. G. Noverre. *Lettres sur la
> Danse, les Ballets et les Arts.*

JEAN LANY

Lany offered pictures opposed to the serious and
demi-caractère styles ; he was supreme in shepherd
parts. This dancer was well versed in everything
appertaining to the execution of a step ; moreover,
owing to the heaviness of his build, he had to rely
on the charms of the style he had chosen, but he
possessed them in the highest degree.

> J. G. Noverre. *Lettres sur la
> Danse, les Ballets et les Arts.*

LOUISE LANY

Mlle. Lany, a pupil of her brother, made her first
appearance at the Opéra on her return from Berlin,
and her *début* was a triumph. She had a superb
figure, a beautiful *ballon*, and executed her dances
to perfection ; she displayed strength, elevation, and
brilliance in all her leaps. But this dancer, having
undergone the harshest training, and having been
continually ill-treated by her brother, had developed
a nervousness undoubtedly the result of her appren-
ticeship. This sense of fear never left her and
deprived her features of the power of expression

which she might have been able to add to the charms
of the most correct execution.

> J. G. Noverre. *Lettres sur la
> Danse, les Ballets et les Arts.*

CHARLES LE PICQ

Charming features, the most slender body, the
easiest and lightest movements, the purest, most
spirited, and most natural precision ; such are the
qualities which distinguish Le Picq. If he does
not dance like God the Father, at least he dances
like the King of Sylphs. He has elasticity and
brilliance. His grace and airiness triumph above
all in *demi-caractère* dancing.

> Grimm. *Correspondance Littéraire.*

CHARLES LE PICQ

Le Picq left Naples a moment to come and see
me at Paris, where I arranged his *début*. The
beautiful proportions of his physique, the nobility
of his features, the captivating harmony of his
movements and the delicate finish of an execution
as astonishing as it was easy, and whose physical
efforts were always masked by gracefulness—so many
perfections secured him the most brilliant success
both at the Court and in the theatre.

> J. G. Noverre. *Lettres sur la
> Danse, les Ballets et les Arts.*

LOUIS NIVELON

Nivelon made his *début* at the Opéra at the same
time as Le Picq and the young dancer was very
well received. Very handsome and of attractive
appearance, he devoted himself to the *demi-caractère*
style. He danced *pas de deux* with grace, his poses
were always tasteful ; his execution was infinitely
soft and smooth ; his straightforwardness, his
devotion to duty, made him the most useful dancer
at the Opera. But advantage was taken of his
amiability and he was made to take parts which

had never been designed for him. His goodwill continually exposed him to unfair comparisons, and the verdict was not always favourable, because he was given parts that he had never learned and then compared with a dancer who had made a special study of them. This facility possessed by Nivelon to be able continually to adapt himself put a stop to his studies in his own style. Too late, he perceived his mistake, and endeavoured to avoid the traps which were continually set for him; it was even sought to force him to do what could not be asked of a *premier danseur*. Worn out with the petty intrigues and secret cliques that dominate the stage, he asked for his discharge. Nivelon lives happy and contented, busying himself with his garden and forming friendships. He has everything required to make friends and keep them.

> J. G. Noverre. *Lettres sur la Danse, les Ballets et les Arts.*

MARGUERITE PESLIN AND MARIE ALLARD

Mlle. Peslin and Mlle. Allard were two dancers in the style known in Italy as grotesque. They achieved marvels of technique, endless *pirouettes* devoid of charm, but both of them, although very buxom, were possessed of truly surprising agility; particularly Mlle. Allard.

> Marie Vigée-Lebrun. *Souvenirs.*

ANNE HEINEL

Heinel, German by extraction, was a superb man in woman's guise; that was how she always impressed me. She was of colossal build, tall in proportion, with feet and hands which did not belie the rest; she had a skin admirable in its firmness and freshness, very fine but large features, with eyes so enormous that they resembled gateways. They were admired. I would have shared in this opinion, subject to its being previously agreed that immensity would henceforth be the standard of beauty. Her mouth, which was small, afforded in my opinion, a ridiculous contrast with the whole.

Mlle. Duthé. *Souvenirs.*

ANNE HEINEL

There is a fine dancer whom Mr. Hobart is to transplant to London ; a Mademoiselle Heinel or Ingle, a Fleming. She is tall, perfectly made, very handsome, and has a set of attitudes copied from the classics. She moves as gracefully slow as Pygmalion's statue when it was coming to life, and moves her leg round as imperceptibly as if she was dancing in the Zodiac. But she is not Virgo.

Horace Walpole, in a letter to the Earl of Strafford, written from Paris, August 25th, 1771.

ANNE HEINEL

She is the most graceful figure in the world, with charming eyes, bewitching mouth, and lovely countenance.

Horace Walpole, in a letter to Sir Horace Mann, written from London, April 21st, 1772.

ANNE HEINEL

This dancer astonished Paris and the Court. Her slim figure, the charm of her features, the perfection and nobility of her dancing, gained for her well-merited applause. I should add that she was the most perfect example of the serious style of dancing.

J. G. Noverre. *Lettres sur la Danse, les Ballets et les Arts.*

GAETANO VESTRIS

Vestris the Elder inherited both Dupré's glorious talent and his nickname ; he was acclaimed the god of dancing ; he equalled his mentor in perfection and surpassed him in versatility and discrimination. Vestris danced *pas de deux* with feeling and style. His frequent visits to Stuttgart incited him to study ; he became a great actor and knew how to embellish with the expressiveness of his miming all my pantomimic poems, in which he played the principal parts. His retirement from the Opéra was a fatal blow to fine dancing which, deprived of that beautiful model, fell into extravagance.

J. G. Noverre. *Lettres sur la Danse, Les Ballets et les Arts.*

MAXIMILIEN GARDEL AND GAETANO VESTRIS CONTRASTED

Gardel and Vestris the Elder were in the first rank. I often saw them dance together, especially in a *chaconne* from one of Grétry's operas, I forget which, a *chaconne* which was the rage of Paris. It was a *pas de trois* in which the dancers pursued Mlle. Guimard, so small and so thin, that it was said they looked like two big dogs quarrelling over a bone. Gardel always seemed to me to be inferior to Vestris the Elder, who was a tall, very handsome man, and perfect in the noble and serious style of dancing. I cannot tell you with what grace he doffed and donned his hat in the honour which precedes the menuet, moreover, all the young ladies of the Court, before being presented, took lessons from him to learn how to make the three courtesies.

Marie Vigée-Lebrun. *Souvenirs.*

MLLE. THÉODORE

I have still to speak of a charming dancer, Mlle. Théodore. She married Dauberval, whose pupil she had been. This dancer was the personification of Terpsichore ; she had freedom, facility, and brilliance. Her *ballon* made her execution so light that, without springing and solely by the elasticity of her insteps, she gave the impression that she never touched the ground.

J. G. Noverre. *Lettres sur la Danse, les Ballets et les Arts.*

MADELEINE GUIMARD

She is as thin as a rake, but how graceful ! How

she rounds her long arms and conceals her pointed elbows ; it is incredible that she should display such perfect taste in her bearing ; there is nothing to suggest the habits of the bad company she keeps. She always has, so it is said, a swarm of admirers ; and, although not virtuous, she can be very difficult. It is imperative to be possessed of a great deal of money, or of an unrivalled beauty, youth, or wit. She is very charitable ; she continually gives money to the parish funds ; and, in winter-time, her servants have strict instructions never to shut the kitchen door against a beggar.

Baronne d'Oberkirch. *Mémoires.*

MADELEINE GUIMARD

Mlle. Guimard attracted the applause of the public from her first appearance to her last ; the Graces had endowed her with their gifts ; she was possessed of every accomplishment and charm. She never courted difficulties, a noble simplicity dominated her dancing ; she danced tastefully and put expression and feeling into all her movements. After having danced the serious style for a long time, she forsook it in order to devote herself to the mixed style which I had created for her and Le Picq. She was inimitable in anacreontic ballets, and, when she retired from the stage, that pleasing style departed with her.

J. G. Noverre. *Lettres sur la Danse, les Ballets et les Arts.*

MADELEINE GUIMARD

Mlle. Guimard had quite another style of talent, her dancing was sketchy ; she only did little steps, but with such graceful movements that the public preferred her to all other dancers ; she was small, slender, very well-made, and, although plain, had such delicate features that at forty-five she looked on the stage no more than fifteen.

Marie Vigée-Lebrun. *Souvenirs.*

MADELEINE GUIMARD

It was in the dance *terre à terre* that Mlle. Guimard delighted a critical audience for over twenty-five years in the gavottes in *Armide*, and in two hundred other dances.   She was always different.   I am not referring only to the charm of the movements of her feet, which were few in comparison with those of her head and body.   Therein lies the perfection of the picture.   She acted comedy as perfectly as light opera.   Her expressive features depicted with ease the emotions she felt or was supposed to feel.

Despréaux.   *Letter to Després*
(*Journal de Paris*, May 7th, 1820).

LISE NOBLET

Noblet's form was perfect ; she could scarcely in other respects be with propriety called handsome. The sparkling vivacity of her black eyes deceived many into a first-night belief that she had more beauty than really belonged to her, but a longer acquaintance showed that her features, though pleasing, were not beautiful.

John Ebers.   *Seven Years of the King's Theatre.*

MLLE. BROCARD

The beauty of this lady made an impression in her favour, which her talents confirmed.   Her dancing was exquisitely graceful, her pantomime exceedingly good, her attitudes perfectly classical, her figure faultless.

John Ebers.   *Seven Years of the King's Theatre.*

FANNY BIAS

Fanny Bias was a dancer of the *demi-caractère*, perfect in those beautiful little half-steps, which, more than any other, correspond to the epithet " twinkling," lavished by poets on the feet of graceful dancers.

Fanny Bias . . . was not beautiful, nor had she the perfection of figure that belonged to Noblet ; but her feet were perfect models, and her style of dancing had an unstudied negligence about it that captivated one unawares.

John Ebers. *Seven Years of the King's Theatre.*

MARIE TAGLIONI

Went to the Opéra last night, when I saw the *début* of the new *danseuse* Taglioni. Hers is a totally new style of dancing ; graceful beyond all comparison, wonderful lightness, an absence of all violent effort, or at least of the appearance of it, and a modesty as new as it is delightful to witness in her art. She seems to float and bound like a sylph across the stage, never executing those *tours de force* that we know to be difficult and wish were impossible, being always performed at the expense of decorum and grace, and requiring only activity for their achievement.

She excited the most rapturous applause, and received it with a " decent dignity," very unlike the leering smiles with which, in general, a *danseuse* thinks it necessary to advance to the front of the proscenium, showing all her teeth, as she lowly courtesies to the audience.

There is a sentiment in the dancing of this charming votary of Terpsichore that elevates it far beyond the licentious style generally adopted by the ladies of her profession, and which bids fair to accomplish a reformation in it.

Lady Blessington. *The Idler in France.*

MARIE TAGLIONI IN PUBLIC AND PRIVATE

Marie Taglioni was not endowed by Nature with any of those qualities which give promise of a dancer and which are considered indispensable for the Opéra stage. She was not beautiful, her figure was a little flat, her arms were long. To see her appear for the first time, at rest, she inspired a deep feeling of sympathy ; her modest demeanour, her downcast eyes, her gentle, open expression, proclaimed an

D

amiable person having the wish to please without any pretensions, one of those rare characters with no harshness in her nature. All this is true as regards the woman.

But the dancer !

She began, she raised those arms which worried us, they were two garlands ; she smiled, she seemed happy ; she was a child leaping in time, as if she had not a care in the world, executing as she played *tours de force* which became miracles of grace. In three bounds she traversed the stage from one end to the other : she flew, she never touched the ground ; her breathing remained untroubled ; her feet, real jewels, appeared as much at home in their satin slippers as those of a pretty farm-girl in her little wooden shoes. And then, when this prodigious flight was ended, she came to the front of the stage, and took up her usual pose, without any grimaces and without any apparent effort. When other dancers have completed their *pas*, they seem to say :

" I hope you are satisfied. I have worked hard to please you and really achieved impossibilities."

Taglioni, on the other hand, invested her being with a simplicity, even an artlessness, which eliminated every suggestion of labour and difficulty ; to see her thus you might imagine that you could do the same things without any difficulty, and that she was only there to amuse herself. Thus she revealed neither fatigue nor nervousness ; nothing detracted from the pleasure and admiration she aroused, you thought no more of her dancing three hours in succession than you would of a bird flying about flowers ; she was certainly destined for the dance. Never did human creature possess such grace and charm.

She it was who first revealed to us the *danse ballonnée*, her skirt almost flew above her head and yet she seemed the personification of modesty. She must be seen to be believed. Who has not seen Taglioni in *Le Dieu et la Bayadère*, in *La Révolte du*

Sérail, and, above all, in *La Sylphide*, is unacquainted
with the poetry of dancing.   Others have unsuccess-
fully sought to equal her without reaching to the
height of that slender and well-attached ankle
which accorded such distinction to her steps.
Her legs were finely-shaped.   As for her feet,
Victor Hugo has recorded their qualities far better
than I could hope to do by autographing a book
he sent her :

A   vos   pieds—à   vos   ailes.

Marie Taglioni has a very even temper which she
retains no matter what the circumstances.   She is
very benevolent ; she is sweet-tempered, calm, and
does not indulge in either extravagancies or tantrums.
Intrigue is unknown to her ; she speaks ill of no one,
she is just and impartial in her judgments, even in
regard to those who have sought to rival her.

She has no more pretensions to fashion than to
staginess.   Once her wings are folded she forgets
the theatre.   She lives like another being.   She does
not boast of her successes.   If the subject is mentioned she does not avoid it, she delights in her success
without any suggestion of vanity or brag.   She is
willing to chat but is not a gossip ; she knows how to
listen.   She willingly admits that in her childhood
she learned nothing but *entrechats* ; she asks questions
and seeks to improve her knowledge.   She has read
a great deal since she became a celebrity ; but she is
not a blue-stocking ; she jokes about herself and
mocks at what she terms her ignorance.

No one seeks retirement and obscurity more than
Mlle. Taglioni.   She lives in her home like a simple
citizeness, and nothing could less resemble an artist's
abode than that quiet house where everything is done
at a certain time and in the same manner.   If you
visited her without knowing on whom you were
calling, you would think she was an ordinary and
unknown mother of a family.   You would see a
comfortable drawing-room with the traditional

piano, and a work-table on which are all the implements of womanly occupation. A tapestry-frame is in one corner, a chair-cover begun by a fairy's hand is stretched upon it. Further away are artificial flowers which she has made; in a room at the side the table is covered with a marvellous cloth—all worked by her. Here are caps, children's clothes, footstools, and boxes; she has embroidered them all. She is hardworking and busies herself in her home from morning to night.

Marie Taglioni has a cheerful character, she animates everyone about her. Family life is cloudless with her. Although she has been much sought after in all the countries she has passed through, she flees society-life which does not appeal to her. She has a sensitive nature and retires within herself. When she lived in Paris in the days of her triumph at the Opéra, she was at home without ceremony every Sunday to artists, journalists, distinguished men of the world, and a very few actresses—she chose them very carefully. There were no exercises in wit at these parties, the time was passed in charades and simple games. The visitors were like children on holiday. They laughed and scampered like urchins, and Mme. la Comtesse Gilbert de Voisins (Taglioni had just been married) led that joyous band with the high spirits of a young girl.

Gala performances and showy clothes bore her. All the same she can dress to perfection. Her manners are beyond criticism. She does not force people to look at her, rather does she keep in the background; there is nothing giddy or extravagant either in her gestures or in her appearance, she would pass unnoticed anywhere. Those who did not know her might pass her twenty years and never guess that she had had all Europe at her feet.

Taglioni is a person worthy of respect, straightforward, with simple tastes. Her needs are very few and she willingly invests her savings. She has never led the life of her profession, she has no desire to shine, and her name is rarely mentioned outside the Opéra.

She has friends and deserves to have them ; she has a good and noble heart. Her nature is not expansive and passionate, it is tender. She is retiring in everything, she hates noise and ostentation. She does good for the love of it, without any expectation of gratitude. She is not extravagant, on the contrary she reckons carefully and does not waste a halfpenny. She is logical and not capricious. In her home there is everything necessary, but nothing superfluous.

Hers is not a sparkling intelligence, but full of common sense ; she has a judgment which can be depended upon. Hers is a positive brain. Her conversation is not remarkable : she says what she wishes to say, she explains herself clearly, she is always understood—she does not indulge in phrases or metaphors.   She has suffered much during her life because she has been lavish with her affections.

She adores children, she loves her mother with whom she has lived constantly.

Mlle. Taglioni is not fashionably dressed ; her clothes are simple like everything about her.   She possesses some very fine jewels and some superb shawls, presents from all the sovereigns of the universe ; she leaves them in her drawers and goes out in plain dresses that no one would ever dream of looking at.

She walks a great deal, she plants trees and flowers.   It is said that she does not regret the stage ; she has, however, been accused of leaving it too late. Dancers, unfortunately, last only as long as roses, and roses last but a little while.

Jacques Raynaud. *Portraits Contemporains.*

FANNY ELSSLER

In 1822 I saw this beautiful person for the first time.   She was originally one of the figurantes at the opera at Vienna, and was at this time about fourteen years of age, and of delicate and graceful proportions. Her hair was auburn, her eyes blue and large, and her face wore an expression of great tenderness.

Capt. Gronow. *Reminiscences and Recollections.*

FANNY ELSSLER

Mlle. Fanny Elssler is tall, supple, and well-formed ; she has delicate wrists and slim ankles ; her legs, elegant and well-turned, recall the slender but muscular legs of Diana, the virgin huntress ; the knee-caps are well-defined, stand out in relief, and make the whole knee beyond reproach. . . .

Another praiseworthy feature is that Mlle. Elssler has rounded and well-shaped arms, which do not reveal the bone of the elbow. . . . Her bosom is full, a rarity among dancers, where the twin hills and mountains of snow so praised by students and minor poets appear totally unknown. Neither can one see moving on her back those two bony triangles which resemble the roots of a torn-off wing.

As to the shape of her head, we must admit that it does not seem to us to be as graceful as it is said to be. Mlle. Elssler is endowed with superb hair which falls on each side of her temples, lustrous and glossy as the two wings of a bird ; the dark shade of her hair clashes in too southern a manner with her typically German features ; it is not the right hair for such a head and body. This peculiarity is disturbing and upsets the harmony of the whole ; her eyes, very black, the pupils of which are like two little stars of jet set in a crystal sky, are inconsistent with the nose, which, like the forehead, is quite German.

Mlle. Elssler has been styled a *Spaniard from the North*, which phrase has been intended as a compliment ; but that is her defect. She is German in her smile, the whiteness of her skin, the shape of her body, the placidity of her forehead ; she is Spanish in her hair, her little feet, her tapering and dainty hands, the somewhat bold curve of her back. In her, two nations and two temperaments are opposed : her beauty would gain were she to decide to be one or the other of these two types. She is pretty, but cross-bred ; she wavers between Spain and Germany. And that same indecision is to be observed in the character of her sex ; her hips are but little developed, her breast does not exceed the fullness of an herm-aphrodite of antiquity ; just as she is a very charming woman, so she might be the handsomest young man in the world.

Théophile Gautier. *Portraits Contemporains.*

FANNY ELSSLER AT NEW YORK

I called yesterday upon Miss Fanny Elssler. She is an exceedingly fascinating person, but not very handsome. Her face has lost its bright bloom, and her complexion appears to be somewhat faded— the result, probably, of the violent muscular exertions which are required in the profession. But her manners are lady-like. She is gay and lively, and altogether the most perfectly graceful lady I have ever seen ; further the deponent saith not.

Philip Hone. *Diary.* (Entry under May 12th, 1840.)

MARIE TAGLIONI AND FANNY ELSSLER CONTRASTED

Fanny Elssler's dancing is quite different from the academic idea, it has a particular character which sets her apart from all other dancers ; it is not the aerial and virginal grace of Taglioni, it is something more human, more appealing to the senses. Mlle. Taglioni is a Christian dancer, if one may make use of such an expression in regard to an art proscribed by the Catholic faith ; she flies like a spirit in the midst of transparent clouds of white muslin with which she loves to surround herself, she resembles a happy angel who scarcely bends the petals of celestial flowers with the tips of her pink toes. Fanny is a quite pagan dancer ; she reminds one of the muse Terpsichore, tambourine in hand, her tunic, exposing her thigh, caught up with a golden clasp ; when she bends freely from her hips, throwing back her swooning, voluptuous arms, we seem to see one of those beautiful figures from Herculaneum or Pompeii which stand out in white relief against a black background, marking their steps with resounding cymbals ; Virgil's line :

Crispum sub crotalo docto movere latus,

involuntarily springs to the mind.   The Syrian slave whom he loved so much to see dancing beneath the pale arbour of the little inn would have had much in common with Fanny Elssler.

> Théophile Gautier.   *Histoire de l'Art Dramatique en France depuis Vingt-Cinq Ans.*

MARIE TAGLIONI CONTRASTED WITH FANNY ELSSLER

The year [1833] which showed us *La Sylphide*, with Madame Taglioni in the prime and perfection of her grace, which introduced an artist so incomparable, in another style, as Madame Fanny Elssler, was in its way a memorable one.

La Sylphide marks a ballet epoch, as a work that introduced an element of delicate fantasy and fairyism into the most artificial of all dramatic exhibitions —one which, to some degree, poetised it.   After *La Sylphide* were to come *La Fille du Danube* and *Giselle* (containing some of Adam's best music), *L'Ombre*, and a score of ballets in which the changes were rung on naiad and on nereid life—on the ill-assorted love of some creature of the elements for some earthly mortal.   The purity and ethereal grace of Mlle. Taglioni's style doubtless suggested the opening of this vein, as it also founded a school of imitators.   Then her mimic powers, however elegant, were limited.   Her face had few changes. Her character dances, as in *Guillaume Tell*, *La Bayadère*, were new and graceful ; but their seduction, piquancy, and national chagrin were to be outdone. When she touched our cold English ground, however,

The Sylph excited as much enthusiasm as the most idolised songstress can now do. . . . While diamond bracelets were flung to her on the stage by magnificent patrons of the art, while the European world of play-goers was ringing with the fascination of the young Swedish artist, she was contented (alternately with one of those creations which filled the theatre) to take such accessory parts as that of the Swiss peasant in Signor Rossini's opera, or the ghostly abbess in M. Meyerbeer's *Robert*.

It was long and late before the star of Mlle. Taglioni waned, before her lightness failed her, before it was whispered that there might be some little sameness in her effects. Even then its wane was accelerated by the growing success in the dancing world of a rival in a style and of a humour totally different—Mademoiselle Fanny Elssler. This last-named woman of genius had to " bide her time " both in Paris and London. Our public, at least, has not room in its heart for two sensations at once. Those who were captivated by the tenderness and the elegance—even when her flights were the boldest —of Mlle. Taglioni, maintained that there was too little of the *semi-reducta Venus* in the presentations of the young, fresh, and bold dancer from Vienna. As to personal attractions, there could be no comparison between the two women. Mlle. Elssler's dignified and triumphant beauty of face and form would have made her remarked whatever dress she wore, in whatever world she appeared. There was more, however, of the Circe than of the Diana in her smile, a quiet if not imperious consciousness of power and accomplishment, a *bravura* of style in her intercourse with the public, which was too keen for some eyes to bear. A mistress of the grand and artificial art of dancing, she possessed many more resources than Mlle. Taglioni. She had studied Héberle closely ; she had gone through every species of exercise which can give firmness and suppleness and the completest concord among all parts of the body, whether the

same was in rapid motion, or flung into these un-
naturally graceful and conventional postures which
in dancing astonish rather than allure the uninitiated.
The exquisite management of her bust and arms (one
of the hardest things to acquire for the dancing) set
her apart from everyone whom I have seen before or
since.   Nothing in execution was too daring for her,
nothing too pointed. If Madame Taglioni flew,
she flashed.   The one floated on to the stage like a
nymph ; the other showered every sparkling fascination round her like a sorceress, with that abundance
which finds enjoyment in its own exercise.   Her
versatility, too, was complete.   She had every
style, every national humour, under her feet : she
could be Spanish for Spaniards, or Russian for
the northerns, or Neapolitan for those who love
the delirious *Tarantella*, with as much variety as
certainty.

The above qualities, however, though great, may
be numbered among those technical ones which
every thoroughly-trained dancer is expected to exhibit
as a matter of course.   But beyond these Mlle.
Elssler as an actress commanded powers of high and
subtle rarity—powers unsuspected during the period
when her rival was queen of the stage, when invention
was set to work principally to fit *her* with proper
occupation.

Henry F. Chorley.   *Thirty
Years' Musical Recollections.*

THERESA AND FANNY ELSSLER

Theresa Elssler suggests at once the notion of one
of the Titanesque Graces.   Her proud crest seems
to aspire to the clouds, which dissolve before the
dainty majesty of her brow.   Fanny Elssler is the
miniature of this fine reality, with a multitude of
smaller beauties that play round her like a halo.   The
scale of her execution is reduced, but her style is the
same, glittering with more minute and dazzling
points, that would be lost in the loftier stature of

her sister. In both, the visible presence of strength is deprived of its physical coarseness by ineffable composure, and that certainty of movement which softens it into a sense of ease. This great power and command of action gives extraordinary luxuriance and freedom to the marvellous evolutions of the dance. The most rapid changes and picturesque attitudes, accomplished at the very extremity of muscular effort, are thus effected without awakening a passing distrust of their complete fulfilment ; so that a series of brilliant measures, which, attempted by others, would be no more than feats of gymnastic skill, are thus achieved with a feeling of inexpressible beauty. Their intertwining action is a triumph of art. Every turn has a regularity and completeness which, apart from its picturesque associations, dispose it into such perfect combinations, that invention can add nothing to its consummate grace. The incessant variety of their motions—the novelty that constantly grows up out of their steps, which have a blinding lustre in their rapidity—fill the eyes with flashing rays, like the perpetual circles that chase each other in some of the freaks of the phantasma. The slightest speck of resting-place suffices to sustain their gyrations ; and they almost seem to realise the fabulous capacity of the angels crowding on the point of a needle. In the dances of the Elsslers there is a strict rhythm, which at once captivates the ear. They ascend and descend, advance and retreat, soar and flutter, with the punctuality of notes delivered in accurate time. When their feet press the ground, they may be said to express music from their touch. Their stately bearing sheds over their performances an abiding charm, that dignifies even those brilliant surprises which sometimes break in upon their loftier movements, like sunny faces smiling suddenly upon us in solitude, and vanishing as fast as they appear. They have originated a new era in their art, and formed a style which is not merely new, but which demands so many various qualities of excellence, that it is hardly too much to say that it is inimitable.

The Monthly Chronicle. July–December, 1838.

CARLOTTA GRISI

Carlotta, despite her Italian origin and name, is fair, or at least light chestnut, she has blue eyes, of an unusual limpidity and softness. Her mouth is small, dainty, childlike, and nearly always tending to a fresh, natural smile, very different from that stereotyped grin usually seen on the lips of actresses. Her complexion is of the rarest delicacy and freshness ; she reminds one of a tea-rose about to blossom. She has a well-proportioned body which, although slender and light, has nothing of that attenuated anatomy which so often makes dancers resemble race-horses in training—all bone and muscle. With her, there is never any sense of weariness or hard work, she is happy to dance for sheer love of it, like a young girl at her first ball ; and, however difficult the thing she has to do, she does it as though it were the merest trifle, which is as it should be ; because in the arts nothing is so disagreeable as a difficulty obviously overcome.

Théophile Gautier. *Portraits Contemporains.*

PAULINE DUVERNAY

Pauline Duvernay was one of the most ravishing women you could wish to see. She was twenty, had charming eyes, an admirably turned leg, and a figure of perfect elegance. As for her dancing, she was full of grace and fire.

Charles Séchan. *Souvenirs d'un*
Homme de Théâtre.

PAULINE DUVERNAY

When I think of Duvernay prancing in as the Bayadère—I say it was a vision of loveliness such as mortal eyes can't see nowadays. How well I remember the tune to which she used to appear !

Kaled used to say to the Sultan : " My Lord, a troop of those dancing and singing girls called Bayadères approaches," and, to the clash of cymbals, and the thumping of my heart, in she used to dance !   There has never been anything like it—never.   There never will be—I laugh to scorn old people who tell me about your Noblet, your Montessu, your Vestris, your Parisot—pshaw, the senile twaddlers !

W. M. Thackeray. *Roundabout Papers.*

CARLOTTA GRISI

This dancer is the only one, since Mlles. Taglioni and Fanny Elssler, who exhibited something like individuality as compared with imitation, or repetition of known effects.   She had not the dancer's face, with its set smile put on to disguise breathless distress and fatigue ; but she looked shy and young and delicate and fresh.   There was something of the briar rose in her beauty.

Henry F. Chorley. *Thirty Years' Musical Recollections.*

LUCILE GRAHN

The Danish dancer is tall, slender, small-jointed, and well-made, and would be prettier still if she did not wear such an obstinate smile.

Théophile Gautier. *Histoire de l'Art Dramatique en France depuis Vingt-Cinq Ans.*

ADELINE PLUNKETT

Mlle. Plunkett is young, pretty, well-formed, with a dainty foot, slender leg, and charming features ; but she is a little delicate for the stage and difficult to see in the distance ; nevertheless, she has all the requisite qualities to become a dancer.

Théophile Gautier. *Histoire de l'Art Dramatique en France depuis Vingt-Cinq Ans.*

SOFIA FUOCO

Mlle. Fuoco is very young ; she is seventeen at

most, as is proved by a certain slenderness of her arms and shoulders. Her features, without being exactly pretty, have a certain attraction and vivacity ; she is happy when dancing and her lips part in a natural smile.

Théophile Gautier.   *Histoire de l'Art Dramatique en France depuis Vingt-Cinq Ans.*

FANNY CERRITO

Fanny Cerrito is well endowed for the stage. She is fair ; her blue eyes have both brilliance and tenderness ; an easy smile illumines her interesting features. She is well built, her arms are soft and rounded, a quality rare among dancers. Her well-developed bosom has none of the scragginess so characteristic of choregraphy ; her leg is slender, and she has a pretty foot. In the matter of physical qualities, she is well fitted to express the poetic fantasies of the writers of themes for ballets. Undines, sylphides, salamanders will not cavil at her rendering of them.

As a dancer, Fanny Cerrito's principal qualities are grace of pose, unusual attitudes, quickness of movement, and the rapidity with which she covers ground ; she bounds and rebounds with an admirable ease and elasticity ; there is a charming grace about her whole body ; her arms, that bugbear of dancers, who listen willingly to the advice of the servant in *Le Malade Imaginaire*, and would discard them as burdensome and useless, curve, bend, and float softly in the air like the pink draperies that flutter about the nymphs in the dark background of the frescoes of Herculaneum.

She radiates a sense of happiness, brilliance, and smiling ease which know neither labour nor weariness. But her very merits are her defects. If facility, freshness, and a youthful manner are present, style and precision are lacking ; and, without wishing at this juncture to enter into the most ridiculous of all pedantries, the pedantry of frivolity, we shall say that she shows signs of lack of training. Nature has done everything for Cerrito ; but even the best of gifts must be developed. An artist of her capability and renown must not let herself be led away by the criticism of dancing-masters, who think they have said everything when they have commented on weak *pointes*, and some position in which the foot is not sufficiently turned out. These little blemishes disappear very quickly in the dazzling whirlwind of that bold, artless, unexpected, and graceful dancing.

> Théophile Gautier. *Histoire de l'Art Dramatique en France depuis Vingt-Cinq Ans.*

FANNY CERRITO

Short of stature, and round in frame, Cerrito is an example of how grace will overcome the lack of personal elegance, how mental animation will convey vivacity and attraction to features which, in repose, are heavy and inexpressive. With a figure which would be too redundant, were it not for its extreme flexibility and abandon, Cerrito is yet a charming artiste, who has honourably earned a high popularity and deservedly retained it.

> Théophile Gautier. *Beauties of the Opera and Ballet.*

CAROLINA ROSATI

A woman of excitable nature, with a slightly satanic and somewhat mournful expression, Rosati excels in strong, noble, and pathetic characters. She is no less excellent in comedy and homely parts. In the rendering of passion she is unrivalled. The most delicate gradations are rendered precisely and clearly in her miming. There is nothing vague in the expression of her thoughts and she seems to endeavour to suppress minor details, having discovered that a few chosen touches produce the most surprising effects. Her gestures are simple, her poses full of grace and harmony.... Ingenious, intelligent in her understanding of character, by turns raging or tender, carried away by despair or spellbound in the ecstasy of a charming dream, she achieved by her miming the same prodigies which Ristori attained with the resources of a more complete art.

Larousse. *Dictionnaire du XIXe Siècle.*

ELIÉ

The ballet of *Gustave III*[1], recalls the name of the dancer-mime Elié, whose death was recently announced in the newspapers, and who contributed much to the success of that ballet. Little noticed up to then, he revealed his worth in a wonderful *pas* in which he danced with two faces ; on one side, dressed as a marquis, he mimed characteristic poses in an affected manner ; then, all of a sudden, he turned about and became a Polichinel, who gave way to the most eccentric and extravagant steps. All Paris rushed to the Opéra to see Elié in this dual dance, so that he became quite a character.

Charles Séchan. *Souvenirs d'un Homme de Théâtre.*

ANGELINA FIORETTI

Of the Italian school, ever ready to dance, essentially graceful and supple, and often given to laughing.

Albert Vizentini. *Derrière la Toile.*

LOUISE AND EUGÉNIE FIOCRE

Here are the two sisters Fiocre, twin Cupids. Louise (the elder, associated with *Pierre de Medicis*) is a plump little person, dark, with a pleasing smile.

Eugénie (the younger, Cupid in *Nemea*) is a fitting model for a sculptor—tall, fair, and well-formed. Only she is too obviously aware of it and always appears to be posing as a model.

Albert Vizentini. *Derrière la Toile.*

ELENA ANDREYANOVA

Mlle. Andreyanova, then, the St. Petersburg *première danseuse*, is a light and agile dancer, with

[1] The ballet occurs in the fifth act of the opera.

a pretty turn of head which recalls Mlle. Taglioni in her youth. It is easy to see that she loves her art and realises its importance to the full. We do not know whether she is a favourite pupil of Taglioni's, but we were soon conscious of that indescribable mixture of artlessness and boldness which contributed so much to the Sylphide's classic charm.

J[ules]. J[anin]. *Journal des Débats.*
Dec. 15. 1845.

EMMA LIVRY

From her first appearance in the *pas* in *Herculanum*, she had shown herself to be a dancer of the first rank, and the attention of the audience had never strayed from her. She belonged to the Taglioni school, which makes of dancing an almost intangible art by reason of its modest grace, chaste reserve, and diaphanous virginity. As one glimpsed through the transparency of her veilings, of which her foot barely raised the hem, she might have been thought to be a happy shade, an elysian apparition at play in a bluish radiance ; she was possessed of imponderable lightness, and her silent flight traversed space without one's hearing the faintest quiver in the air. In the ballet, the only one, alas, that she created, she took the part of a butterfly, and this was not a commonplace *rôle*. She could imitate a butterfly's fantastic and charming flight, and the way in which it alights on a flower without weighing it down.

Théophile Gautier. *Portraits Contemporains.*

WILHELMINA SALVIONI

Inferior in graceful dancing, she had her revenge in mimed scenes, where her native passions, her inclinings, her energetic bounds, her mute sadness, and her very interesting and very intelligent moments of dramatic abandon earned her a substantial and merited success. A little hard-featured, but possessed of the divine fire, Mlle. Salvioni excels in *ballon*, but opens her mouth too much; she customarily sings *Plaisir d'Amore*, Martini's old song, and always goes into the house to applaud her bosom friend, Mlle. Fioretti.

Albert Vizentini.   *Derrière la Toile*.

LEONTINE BEAUGRAND

A worker, very strong in execution and very correct, the only dancer at the Opéra who knows how to dance a *variation* played on the violins. It is marvellous to see her follow the strokes of the bow and mark the time with her little feet with the most praiseworthy rhythm, precision, and grace. Always in a rage and in a state of nerves which makes her little nose look longer, she has no other characteristic than that of adoring pralines.

Albert Vizentini.   *Derrière la Toile*.

ROSITA MAURI

Pretty? Better than pretty, adorable, with a prettiness that goes to your head. Her face is a trifle thin, her mouth large, her complexion the tint of a Spanish lemon. But what a fire gleams in her eyes. What a smile there is on her fresh lips and flashing teeth. And what a body, moulded by the *maillot*. A statuette of slender and pure proportions, but an animated, living statuette which, at the least movement, by a gift of nature, betrays its vivacity, suppleness, strength, and grace.

François Coppée.   *A propos d'un Ballet*
(*Figaro Illustré*, February, 1895).

NADEZHDA BOGDANOVA

The week I arrived in Petersburg was the last of the season of the Grand Opera; and I had the pleasure of enjoying some toe-pointed stanzas of the poetry of motion as rendered by the agile limbs of the renowned Russian dancer, Mademoiselle Bagdanoff. The Russians are deliriously proud of this favoured child of Terpsichore. . . . The Bagdanoff is their Alpha and Omega as a dancer. Last spring she was more the rage than ever. Her portrait, lithographed, was in all the print-sellers' windows, with a sprawling autograph at the base, and a German epigraph at the summit : " *In lebe immer die selbe,*" " In love always the same. . . ." I saw Mademoiselle Bagdanoff, and didn't like her. Have I not seen Her (with a large H) dance ? She flung her limbs about a great deal ; and in dancing, as in love, she was *immer die selbe*—always the same. It afterwards fell out that from the fumes of that great witch's cauldron of Russian gossip, the Samovar, I distilled a somewhat curious reason for the immense popularity of the Bagdanoff.

The imperial government granted her a ticket of leave, or passport for foreign travel, just before the war with the allied powers broke out. Nadiejda went abroad, remained two years, and came back at last, radiant, as Mademoiselle Bagdanoff, of the Académie Impériale de Musique at Paris. She had stormed the Rue Lepelletier ; she had subdued the Parisians ; she had vanquished the stubborn hearts and claque-compelling, white-gloved palms of those formidable three first rows of *fauteuils d'orchestre*, courted and dreaded by all cantatrice, by all ballerine. In a word she had triumphed ; but it was never exactly ascertained in what ballet she had made her *début*. It was certain, however, that she had been engaged at the Académie, and that her engagement had been rescinded during the war time ; the manager having, with fiendish ingenuity, endeavoured to seduce her into dancing in a ballet whose plot was inimical to Russian interests. But, the fair Nadiejda, patriotic and fearless, indignantly refused to betray her country and her Czar. She tore her engagement into pieces ; she stamped upon it ; she gave the directors of the Académie Impériale a piece of her mind : she demanded her passports, and danced back to St. Petersburg—there to be fêted, and caressed, and braceleted, and ear-ringed, and bouqueted,

and re-engaged at the Balschoï Teatr' at a higher
salary.

George Augustus Sala.   *A Journey due North.*

MARIE S. PETIPA

Marie Petipa's dancing is full of a captivating
grace and roguishness. She is lighter and livelier
than a bird. She is the first butterfly of spring, the
butterfly which hovers about every flower yet alights
on none. Her grace is quite artless, it is not studied,
but natural. In watching her dance and describe
that multitude of *arabesques* on the stage, which
would form a curious pattern could they be preserved, we ask ourselves if that fantasy is not
improvised and the result of a dancer's caprice
born that very night, and which will alter on the
morrow. . . .

Her features are in continual harmony with the
action ; her animated and emphatic gestures are
always in keeping with the plot, her arms are not a
balancing-pole, they are *alive* ; her body has none of
those impossible jerkings of the hip which captivate
admirers of Spanish dancing, but which achieve
nothing from want of attempting too much ; her
smile is not fixed on her lips, it is in her eyes, her
teeth, the roses of her cheeks ; lastly, what is a rarity,
she does not dance because she is a dancer, but for
pleasure, for love of it. . . .

Marie Petipa's style is Italian like that of Ferraris,
Fuoco, and Carlotta ; she shines in the *danse taquetée*
rather than in the *danse ballonnée*. . . . In place of
bounding like Emma Livry, the Russian *danseuse*
prefers to describe all kinds of *arabesques* in the most
novel and delicate manner, two inches from the
Opéra stage, which her little feet—like two wings—
graze without resting there. But the dancer's
charm and skill reside less in those coquettish, bird-
like flutterings close to the ground than in the
indescribable ease and grace which emanate from
her whole body. Marie Petipa *dances with her arms*,

in place of using them like a stiff and awkward means of balance.

That constitutes the originality of her dancing, the novel piquancy of her style. When she encircles space with her two supple and loving arms you seem to see a hamadryad embracing a god who has disguised himself as a cloud.

Lemercier de Neuville. *Marie Petipa.*

VERA TREFILOVA

Mme. Vera Trefilova, whom Paris applauded yesterday for the first time, is a perfect dancer. I particularly abhor national vainglory, but why should I not say that Trefilova was one of the greatest glories of the Imperial Russian Ballet? Her technique is perfect, but she does not regard it as a form of abstract gymnastics ; it is the complete expression of a harmonious whole. In her *adage* the play of the curves and perpendiculars is of an unparalleled purity, she unfolds like an opening flower. Her control of line is so delicate and discreet in its precision that the spectator never suspects the difficulties overcome. Dizzy bounds are not for her, nor great, passionate dartings. Pavlova is the bird, she is the flower. She is at once an admirable instrument and a musician—a dancing Stradivarius.

André Levinson. *La Danse au Théâtre.*

ANNA PAVLOVA

Her body was ideally formed for dancing. She had a slender torso and lovely arms ; and her legs and feet, particularly the insteps, were superb. Her hands, however, were a little large for her arms, and the fingers inclined to be thick ; but when she danced she managed them so skilfully that the hands seemed delicate and the fingers tapering. Her face was pale and oval, her forehead high, her hair dark and drawn close to the head ; her nose was aquiline, her cheek-bones high, her eyes large and the colour of " ripe, dark brown cherries." Her head was beautifully poised on a swan-like neck ; her expression was part elfin, part malicious, part imperious, and it could be as changeable as the very face of nature. Her body was a perfect instrument of expression, it would instantly respond to the mood of a dance, just as a tuning-fork vibrates to a blow.

C. W. Beaumont. *Anna Pavlova.*

MAESTRO CECCHETTI AT HOME

I shall always remember those evenings at Wardour Street. Both Cecchetti and his wife were kindness personified. They had nothing of the lofty airs and graces which characterise petty talents ; every visitor, whether she was a little child learning her five positions, or a *première danseuse* of international reputation, received the same genial welcome. No sooner did one cross the threshold than Madame would proffer a box of chocolates or a jar of biscuits, or Cecchetti would pour out a glass of vermouth. Then he would talk while Madame sat sewing by the fire ; and presently their cat, Mami, would scramble up on the table and listen with eager ears.

Few teachers can have been more loved by their pupils than was Cecchetti. He was always ready to play father-confessor to them all. They sought his advice on both private and business affairs, and, leaning back, with hands together and fingers touching in the classical pose of Sherlock Holmes marshalling his deductions, he would deliver judgment like a second Solomon. He was always plain-spoken, and those who had not known him long and sought his sympathy to alleviate the consequences of some misdeed were speedily disillusioned.

C. W. Beaumont. *Enrico Cecchetti.*

VASLAV NIJINSKY

His half-closed eyes gave an extraordinary, fascinating expression to his face. His features were decidedly Mongolian, and the almond-shaped eyes were a dark brown, although on the stage they seemed a dark blue or green.   He was of medium height and very muscular, but on the stage he seemed tall and slender.   Even his physical being seemed to change according to the part he danced. . . .

Vaslav had a perfectly proportioned body. He weighed almost one hundred and thirty pounds. His legs were so muscular that the hard cords stood out on his thighs like bows. With his unusually powerful arms, controlled by the highest technique, he could pick up and lift his partners with such ease that it seemed as if he only held a doll of straw.   He did not, like other male dancers, support the girl with both hands on her hip, but with one single arm he raised her straight from his side.

Romola Nijinsky. *Nijinsky*.

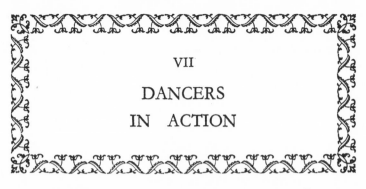

VII

DANCERS
IN ACTION

MARIE SALLÉ IN " L'EUROPE GALANTE "

That dancer appeared in the midst of her rivals, with the graces and desires of a young odalisque who has designs on her lord's heart. Her dance was formed of all the pretty poses such a passion can express. She developed it by degrees ; one read in her expression a whole range of emotions ; one saw her hesitating between fear and hope ; but, at the moment when the sultan gives the handkerchief to his favourite wife, her whole being quickly underwent a change. She tore herself away from the stage with that degree of despair, characteristic of tender and passionate beings, which is expressed only in moments of utter dejection.

Cahusac. *La Danse Ancienne et Moderne.*

MARIE CAMARGO IN " LES FÊTES VENETIENNES "

I saw a *danseuse* who bounded like a fury, cutting *entrechats* to right and left and in all directions, but scarcely rising from the ground ; yet she was received with fervent applause.

Casanova. *Mémoires.*

LOUIS DUPRÉ IN " LES FÊTES VENETIENNES " (1750)

Patu was most anxious to take me to the Opéra in order to witness the effect produced upon me by the performance, which must truly astonish an Italian. The opera given was *Les Fêtes Venetiennes* (ballet by Danchet, music by Campra)—a title full of interest for me. We went for our forty *sous* to the pit, in which, although the audience was standing, the company was excellent ; for this style of entertainment was the favourite amusement of the French.

After a symphony, very good of its kind, and played by an excellent orchestra, the curtain rises, and I see a beautiful scene representing the piazzetta of St. Mark, as seen from the Island of St. George; but I am shocked to see the ducal palace on my left, and the tall steeple on my right, that is to say the very reverse of reality. I began to laugh at this comical and disgraceful mistake, and Patu, to whom I explained the reason for my laughter, had to laugh too. The music, although very fine in the old style, at first amused me on account of its novelty, then bored me. The harmony soon wearied me with its constant and tedious monotony, and by the shrieks given out of place. The harmony of the French replaces—at least they think so—the Greek harmony and our recitative which they dislike, but which they would delight in if they understood Italian.

The action of the opera was limited to a day in the carnival, when the Venetians are wont to promenade masked on the piazza of St. Mark. There were gallants, procuresses, and prostitutes devising all sorts of intrigues ; the costumes were quaint and erroneous, but the whole was amusing. What I could not help laughing at, and it was truly a curious sight for a Venetian, was when I saw the Doge, attended by twelve Councillors, appear on the stage, all dressed in the most odd cloaks, and dancing a *grand passacaille*. Suddenly the pit gave vent to a loud clapping of hands at the appearance of a tall, well-proportioned dancer, wearing a mask and an enormous black wig, the ends of which went halfway down his back, and dressed in a robe, open in front and reaching to his heels. Patu said, almost reverently : " It is the inimitable Dupré." I had heard of him before, and became attentive. I saw that fine figure coming forward with measured steps, and when the dancer had arrived in front of the stage, he slowly raised his rounded and graceful arms, opened, extended and closed them, moved his feet with precision and lightness, took a few small steps, made some *battements* and *pirouettes*, and disappeared like a summer breeze. The whole had not lasted half a minute. Applause and shouts of " Bravo " burst from every part of the house ; I was astonished, and asked my friend the reason for it.

" We applaud the grace of Dupré and the divine harmony of his movements. He is now sixty years of age, and those who saw him forty years ago say that he is always the same."

" What ? Has he never danced in a different style ? "

" He could not have danced in a better one, for his style is perfect, and what can you want above perfection ? "

" Nothing, save it be relative perfection."

" But here it is absolute. Dupré always does the same thing, and every day we fancy we see it for the first time. Such is the power of the good and beautiful, of the true and sublime, which speak to the soul. His dance is true harmony, the real dance, of which you have no idea in Italy."

At the end of the second act, Dupré appeared again, still wearing a mask, and danced to a different tune, but in my opinion doing exactly the same as before. He advanced to the very footlights, and stopped an instant in a most beautiful pose. Patu wanted to force my admiration, and I gave way. Suddenly every one around me exclaimed :

" Look ! Look ! He is growing bigger."

And in truth he was like an elastic body which, in stretching itself, would get larger ; I made Patu very happy by telling him that Dupré was truly graceful in all his movements.

Casanova. *Mémoires.*

GAETANO AND AUGUSTE VESTRIS

Vestris the elder executed the *pirouette* far better

than his son, but he did not abuse his ability ; he made you wish for more. Nowadays, that embellishment of dancing has become its principal feature. The Vestris of to-day does not execute his *pirouettes* smoothly ; he turns with an extraordinary velocity and when the threatened displacement of the centre of gravity warns him of a possible fall, he stops himself by a strong stamp of the feet. If this last be not a marvel of balance, it is certainly a miracle of skill, prudence, and necessity."

J. G. Noverre. *Lettres sur la Danse, les Ballets et les Arts.*

AUGUSTE VESTRIS

Vestris the elder was succeeded by Vestris the younger, the most amazing dancer you could wish to see, because he was at once graceful and aerial. Although our dancers of to-day are not chary of their *pirouettes*, it is certain that none of them will ever achieve as many as he did, then all at once he soared upwards in so prodigious a fashion that he seemed to be endowed with wings.

Marie Vigée-Lebrun. *Souvenirs.*

AUGUSTE VESTRIS AT LYON
April 29th, 1790

The curtain rose. The comedy, *Les Plaideurs*,[1] was given. I could only catch half the words as I paid less attention to the play than to the persons who kept continually coming in and going out of my box. Hardly was the curtain lowered than from all quarters there streamed on the stage actors and actresses in undress, *danseurs* and *danseuses*, and so on.

Some placed their arms round each other's waists and began to dance, others laughed, and others called out ; it was a new piece ! Vestris, dressed like a shepherd, gambolled like a sportive goat. The orchestra struck up again, the heroes of the drama

[1] By Jean Racine.

disappeared, the curtain rose, and the ballet commenced. Vestris appeared. Thunders of applause re-echoed from all parts of the house. In very truth this dancer has the most marvellous talent. He has his soul in his legs, notwithstanding all the conjectures of the students of human nature who seek for that soul in the tissues of the brain. What features ! What suppleness ! What balance ! I never thought that a dancer could afford me such delight. In such wise every art carried to perfection is balm to the soul. The applause from the Frenchmen overwhelmed the music. In the guise of an enraptured lover, whose languorous sighs and beating heart mingled with those of his sweetheart, Vestris disappeared from the view of the audience, embraced his shepherdess, and threw himself upon a little bench to recover his breath. Followed a meaningless comedy in one act. Then came a new ballet. Vestris reappeared and immediately acclamations greeted every movement of his legs. . . .

The ballet ended and the curtain was lowered. The stalls, boxes, and pit, all the spectators with one unanimous voice began to shout : " Stay here, Vestris, stay here ! " The cries went on for several minutes. The curtain rose again and Vestris came forward. What a modest demeanour ! What charm in all his bearing ! What bows ! He held his hat against his heart. One was obliged to stop up one's ears, so overwhelming was the applause. Vestris paused. All at once every one was quiet. You could have heard a grasshopper chirrup.

Vestris : " My leave of absence from Paris is for one month only. That month has expired and now I must depart, but——"

Here his voice broke, he looked upwards and seemed to collect his strength. Terrifying thunders of applause ! Suddenly all was quiet again.

Vestris : " As a proof of my gratitude for the kindness with which you have honoured me, I shall dance once more to-morrow."

A tremendous " Bravo ! " mingled with unanimous applause and the curtain was lowered. The enthusiasm was so great that at that moment the fickle French were quite capable of proclaiming Vestris their dictator.

N. M. Karamzin. *Voyage en France.*

MADELEINE GUIMARD AS NICETTE IN " LA CHERCHEUSE D'ESPRIT "

She invested the part of Nicette with so fine, so exact, so delicate, so piquant a range of shades, that the most skilful poetry could not have rendered the same characters with greater wit, delicacy, and truth. All her *pas*, all her movements, were distinguished by their softness and harmony, a sure and picturesque combination. Her simplicity is artless without being foolish, her natural grace, unaffectedly concealed, develops by degrees and pleases without any sense of importunity. How animated she becomes under the soft rays of feeling. She resembles a rosebud which is seen to open, escape from the fettering tendrils, tremble, and flower. We have seen nothing so delightful and so perfect in this style of mime.

Grimm. *Correspondance Littéraire.*

LISE NOBLET AS NINA IN " NINA "

Nina is a young woman loving and beloved. An obstacle apparently permanent to the current of her affection, deprives her of her senses ; and never was the touching sadness of the worst of maladies more truly delineated than in the mute eloquence of Noblet's performance. The madness of Nina is not the phrenzied excitement of ungovernable despair, but the melancholy estrangement of a mind retaining, in its ruin, the sweetness and benevolence of its unshaken state. In pourtraying the workings of this affliction, not a gesture of this affliction, not a movement of Noblet was idly wasted. Everything was true to nature—everything contributed to the feeling of the piece. Her countenance, expressive as her action was graceful, kept time to every inflection of feeling, and harmonized with all the speaking graces of her deportment.

John Ebers. *Seven Years of the King's Theatre.*

MARIE TAGLIONI AS FLORA IN " FLORE ET ZÉPHYRE "

After the opera, the much-talked-of Taglioni came floating on the stage in the part of *Flora* in the ballet of *Zéphyr et Flora.* For once fame has not overstepped our anticipations. Signora Taglioni is the most perfect specimen of grace and elegance, as a dancer, we ever beheld. Her movements are all a series of classical studies. Not only does it seem a matter of perfect indifference whether she be standing on one foot or on two feet, but every evolution is accomplished with such extraordinary ease, and with the airiness of thistledown, that it would scarcely have increased our wonder and delight had she ascended like a spirit.

The Examiner, June 6th, 1830.

MARIE TAGLIONI

The step and mien of Taglioni are as soft and touching as the beatific visions of some of our old saints. . . . Taglioni's elasticity is even more remarkable than that of the Elsslers, because it is not so apparent. We are not made aware of it by any effort to display it. She floats like a blush of light before our eyes : we cannot perceive the subtle means by which she contrives, as it were, to disdain the earth, and to deliberate her charming motions in the air. Whichever way she turns, there is an expression of beauty—a figure, which, could it be fixed in any of its phases, would convey an embodied sentiment to the imagination. Her dance is an acted poem, sparkling with images, which, reduced to words would resemble the brilliant conceits of Carew or Suckling ; but which, in this tangible and fugitive shape, take an appropriate and congenial place, invulnerable to criticism. She achieves the office of wings without their incumbrance. Her sweetness and gentleness have a wooing tone, which breathes from her with no more external appearance than the aroma from flowers. There are no languishing arts in her manner, yet she sometimes seems to fade away, like a gossamer caressed by the winds. There is this peculiarity in Taglioni—that you can describe her only through the emotions she causes. You cannot separate her from them, and paint a portrait ; but must embellish it with the accessories that, springing out of your own sensations, appear to be essential to the truth. She has something of the effect of a tradition from the East, invested with spells and inspired with fairy gifts ; a legend of miracles to which you willingly subscribe ; a delicious fiction, recreated in life, and rendered a thousand times more fascinating than before by the vital warmth suffused throughout its articulation.

The Monthly Chronicle. July–December, 1838.

MARIE TAGLIONI IN " LA GITANA "

I had not seen Taglioni since the first representation of the *Sylphide*, eight or nine years ago at Paris. Last night I was at the opera, and saw her in *La Gitana*, and except that her limbs are the least in the world rounder and fuller, she is, in person, absolutely unchanged. I can appreciate now, better than I could then (when opera dancing was new to me), what it is, that gives this divine woman the right to her proud title of *La Déesse de la Danse*. It is easy for the Elsslers and Augusta, and others who are said to be only second to her, to copy her flying steps, and even to produce by elasticity of limb the beautiful effect of touching the earth, like a thing afloat, without being indebted to it for the rebound. But Taglioni alone *finishes* the step or the *pirouette*, or the arrowy bound over the scene, as calmly, as accurately, as faultlessly as she begins it. She floats out of a *pirouette* as if, instead of being made giddy, she had been lulled by it into a smiling and childlike dream, and instead of trying herself and her aplomb (as is seen in all other dancers, by their effort to recover composure), it had been the moment when she had rallied and been refreshed. The smile, so expressive of enjoyment in her own grace, which steals over Taglioni's lips when she does a difficult step, seems communicated in an indefinable languor, to her limbs. You cannot fancy her fatigued when, with her peculiar softness of motion, she courtesies to the applause of an enchanted audience, and walks lightly away. You are never apprehensive that she has undertaken too much. You never detect as you do in all other dancers, defects slurred over adroitly and movements that, from their anticipating the music of the ballet, are known by the critical eye to cover some flaw in the step, from giddiness or loss of balance. But, oh, what a new relation bears the music to the dance, when the spirit of grace replaces her companions in the ballet ! Whether the motion seems born of the music, or the music floats out of her dreamy motion, the enchanted gazer might be embarrassed to know.

In the new ballet of *La Gitana*, the music is based upon the mazurka. The story is the old one of the child of a *grandee* of Spain, stolen by gypsies, and recovered by chance in Russia. The gradual stealing over her of music which she had heard in her childhood was the finest piece of pantomimic acting I ever saw. But there is one dance, the Cachuca, introduced at the close of the ballet, in which Taglioni has enchanted the world anew. It could only be done by herself ; for there is a succession of flying movements expressive of alarm, in the midst of which she alights and stands poised upon the points of her feet, with a look over her shoulder of *fierté* and animation possible to no other face, I think, in the world. It was like a deer standing with expanded nostril and neck uplifted to its loftiest height, at the first scent of his pursuers in the breeze. It was the very soul of swiftness embodied in a look ! How can I describe it to you !

N. P. Willis. *Famous Persons and Famous Places.*

FANNY ELSSLER AS ALCINE IN " LA TEMPETE "

The talent of the newcomer differed completely from that of Taglioni ; she danced with a roguish and provocative grace which had nothing in common with the classic style of the *prima ballerina*. Elegant, graceful, light, not given to great leaps, but dancing her *pas* with the greatest care and an exquisite finish, she executed a trill of *battements* as Paganini would have played them on his violin. It may be added that she not only danced to admiration, but was also very pretty.

Charles Séchan. *Souvenirs d'un Homme de Théâtre.*

FANNY ELSSLER IN " LE DIABLE BOITEUX "

She comes forward in her pink satin *basquine* trimmed with wide flounces of black lace ; her skirt, weighted at the hem, fits tightly over the hips ; her slender waist boldly arches and causes the diamond ornament on her bodice to glitter ; her leg, smooth as marble, gleams through the frail mesh of her silk stocking ; and her little foot at rest seems but to await the signal of the music. How charming she is with her big comb, the rose behind her ear, her lustrous eyes and her sparkling smile ! At the tips of her rosy fingers quiver ebony castanets. Now she darts forward ; the castanets begin their sonorous chatter. With her hand she seems to shake down great clusters of rhythm. How she twists, how she bends ! What fire ! What voluptuousness ! What precision ! Her swooning arms toss about her drooping head, her body curves backwards, her white shoulders almost graze the ground. What a charming gesture ! Would you not say that in that hand which seems to skim the dazzling barrier of the footlights, she gathers up all the desires and all the enthusiasm of the spectators ?

We have seen Rosita Diez, Lola, and the best dancers of Madrid, Seville, Cadiz, and Granada ; we have seen the gitanas of Albaicin ; but nothing approaches that Cachuca danced by Elssler.

Théophile Gautier. *Les Beautés de l'Opéra.*

FANNY ELSSLER IN " LA GIPSY "

Mlle. Fanny Elssler in the part of Sarah (the gipsy) has surpassed herself. She has combined Florinda and Fenella ; the " *Pas de la Cracovienne* " affords her a triumph which will make the ballet's fortune. She dances in the most coquettish and roguish costume that could be imagined : an officer's tunic sparkling with buttons and a *vivandière's* skirt, boots with steel spurs, and a black necktie framing a delightful chin—the whole crowned with a triumphant, sprightly little plume, the prettiest you ever saw. It is impossible to describe this dance : it is rhythmic precision mingled with a charming ease, a muscular and bounding agility which cannot be imagined ; the metallic clicking of the spurs, a kind of castanets on the heels, emphasises each step and gives the dance a quality of joyous vivacity which is quite irresistible.

Théophile   Gautier.   *Histoire   de   l'Art Dramatique en France depuis Vingt-Cinq Ans.*

FANNY ELSSLER IN " LA GIPSY "

The Bolero . . . was allotted to a scene where the gipsy girl compels her sulky mates to dance. When she appeared on the stage of Paris the folk lay couched in fifties, huddled together in their wild and picturesque clothes, as only the French stage managers know how to group forms and colours. How she moved hither and thither, quick and bright as a torch, lighting up one sullen heap of tinder after another, gradually animating the scene with motion, till at last the excited rout of vagabonds trooped after her with the wild vivacity of a chorus of bacchanals, made a picture of many pictures, the brightness and spirit of which stand almost alone in the gallery of similar ones. There have been Gitanas, Esmeraldas, Mignons by the score, but no Gipsy to approach Mlle. Fanny Elssler.

In the next act of the same ballet came the scene of the minuet danced by the heroine to gain time, and to distract attention from her lover in concealment hard by, whose life was perilled. . . . Few things have been seen more fearful than the cold measured grace of Mlle. Fanny Elssler in this juncture, than the manner in which every step was watched, every gesture allowed its right time, so that neither flurry nor faltering might be detected, than the set smile, the vigilant ear, the quivering lip controlling itself. It is in moments like these that genius rises above talent.

Henry F. Chorley. *Thirty Years'*
Musical Recollections.

CARLOTTA GRISI IN " LA PÉRI "

At once precise and intrepid, Carlotta Grisi's dancing has a quite special style ; it does not resemble the dancing of either Taglioni or Elssler ; each one of her poses, each one of her movements, is stamped with the seal of originality. How wonderful to be new in an art so limited ! This *pas* includes a certain fall which will soon be as famous as the Niagara Falls. The audience wait for it in awed curiosity. At the moment when the vision is about to end, the Peri falls from the top of a cloud into her lover's arms. If it were only a *tour de force*, we should not mention it ; but this perilous leap forms a group so full of grace and charm that it suggests a dove's feather drifting downwards, rather than a human being leaping from a platform.

Théophile Gautier. *Histoire de l'Art*
Dramatique en France depuis Vingt-Cinq Ans.

CARLOTTA GRISI IN " LA JOLIE FILLE DE GAND."

How she flies, how she rises, how she soars ! How

at home she is in the air ! When, from time to time, the tip of her little white foot skims the ground, it is easy to see that it is out of pure good nature, so as not to drive to despair those who have no wings. We must say that the music of this *pas* is deliciously original ; peals of sparkling notes burst like rockets through the orchestral arrangement, affording a ravishing imitation of those Flemish clocks which inspired Victor Hugo to write a pretty piece of poetry in *Les Rayons et les Ombres*. In fact, Carlotta resembles the ethereal dancer whom the poet sees descend and ascend the crystal staircase of melody in a deep-toned mist of light ! She succeeds without a quiver in attaining the last rung of that ladder of silver filigree which the composer has built for her, as if to defy her lightness, and the public, amazed, furiously applauded her when she came down again, already consoled for the loss of Taglioni, now in Russia in the snow, and of Fanny Elssler, who is in America, near the fires of the Equator. It is impossible to dance with greater perfection, vigour, and grace, with a profounder sense of rhythm and time, with happier or more smiling features. No fatigue, no effort ; no perspiration or gasping ; these wonders accomplished, Carlotta went to sit beneath the great noble trees of the principal square in Ghent, like a young lady who has just danced a *contredanse* in a drawing-room.

Théophile Gautier. *Histoire de l'Art Dramatique en France depuis Vingt-Cinq Ans.*

SOFIA FUOCO IN " BETTY "

Mlle. Fuoco, who makes her *début* in this ballet, bears a name of happy augury—*fire !* It might have been invented for her. This pretty dancer hails from Milan, which has already given us Carlotta Grisi.

From her first appearance, Mlle. Sofia Fuoco made a distinct impression. She has the merit of originality, so rare in the dance, a limited art if ever there was one ; she does not remind one of either Taglioni, Elssler, Carlotta or Cerrito.

Her *pointes* in particular are astounding ; she executes the whole of an *écho* without once lowering her heel to the ground. Her feet are like two steel arrows rebounding from a marble pavement ; not a moment of weakness, not a vibration, not a tremor ; that inflexible toe never betrays the light body it supports.

Other dancers have been said to have wings, to have roamed the air amid clouds of muslin ; Mlle. Fuoco flies too, but grazing the ground with the tip of her nail, alive, quick, dazzling in her rapidity.

Dancing, it will be said, does not consist entirely of *pointes* and *taquetés*. True, but, in everything executed by Mlle. Fuoco, we have remarked that neatness, that finish, that precision which are to the dance what style is to poetry ; we also believe that she possesses other qualities, in a lesser degree, undoubtedly, but sufficient.

Théophile Gautier. *Histoire de l'Art Dramatique en France depuis Vingt-Cinq Ans.*

CAROLINA ROSATI IN " LE CORSAIRE "

As the leading spirit of this short, graphic drama, Rosati had won the highest honours in Paris, both as *danseuse* and mime. She now came to the support of Her Majesty's Theatre, bringing with her all her talent and all her witcheries. She danced—she acted. Her ethereal bounds across the stage were once more marvels of that apparently effortless power which constituted one of her distinguishing charms. By turns sporting with a cajoling grace, which was the very poetry of coquetry, and bursting forth into melodramatic vigour when the exigencies of the stirring story demanded a more powerful display, she proved herself a pantomimist worthy of the experienced Italian mimic, Ronzani, who acted the Conrad to her Medora.

Benjamin Lumley. *Reminiscences of the Opera.*

ROSITA MAURI IN " LA KORRIGANE "

La Mauri is divine, seen from the audience with or without the aid of opera-glasses. Indeed, I regard it as one of the greatest events in my life as a dramatist to have seen that extraordinary artist, that ethereal being who after a prodigious bound—I put in badly —after soaring in the air, returned to the stage so, lightly, so delicately, that you could not hear a sound, no more than when a bird descends and alights on a twig.

La Mauri is dancing personified. To the trials of rehearsal, so tedious and wearing for all the artistes, but particularly exhausting for the *prima ballerina* who must expend so much strength and dexterity, La Mauri brought a kind of physical enthusiasm, a kind of joyous delirium. You felt that she loved to dance for nothing, from instinct, for the love of dancing, even in a dark and empty theatre. She whinnied and darted like a young foal ; she soared and glided in space like a wild bird ; and, in her sombre and somewhat wild beauty, there is something of both the Arab steed and the swallow.

François Coppée. *A propos d'un Ballet* (*Figaro Illustré*, February, 1895).

PIERRINA LEGNANI'S FAMOUS 32 FOUETTÉS

This Italian *ballerina*, on her first appearance in Petersburg, won all hearts, and for over ten years successfully held the stage as a *prima ballerina assoluta*. By no means pretty and rather short of stature, she possessed great charm and grace ; and these qualities, together with marvellous brilliancy of execution, silenced all the antagonists of the Italian school. . . .

One of her *tours de force* was 32 "*fouettés*." It has since been mastered by other dancers, but then if was only done by Legnani. The step was not unlike an acrobatic exercise and its presentation savoured of the circus, by the deliberate suspense preceding it. Legnani walked to the middle of the stage and took an undisguised preparation. The conductor, his baton raised, waited. Then a whole string of vertiginous *pirouettes*, marvellous in their precision and brilliant as diamond facets, worked the whole audience into ecstasies. Academically, such an exhibition of sheer acrobatics was inconsistent with purity of style ; but the feat, as she performed it, had something elemental and heroic in its breathless daring. It overwhelmed criticism.

Thamar Karsavina. *Theatre Street.*

VASLAV NIJINSKY AND THAMAR KARSAVINA IN " LE SPECTRE DE LA ROSE "

From the garden comes a gentle breeze laden with the fragrance of roses, and into the room steps a young girl, sweet and demure in her high-cut ball dress of creamy white, over which is fastened a little cloak. Out of her closely-drawn chiffon bonnet peeps her pretty face. In her hand she holds a rose, fearful lest her tiny fingers even should crumple its fragile beauty. She raises the rose to her lips. What secret does it hold, this lover's token ? She gazes at it with downcast eyes. Surely it is not wrong to be loved ? Her lips quiver and seem to frame his name. She glances round the well-known room ; so friendly, so dear to her with all its innocent treasures. How tired she looks, now that her face is upraised. She throws off her wrap and walks to her beloved arm-chair. With a sigh of content she sinks into it. Her eyelids droop and close. She is asleep. Her hands fall and the rose escapes through her limp fingers, caresses her dress, and falls to the floor.

The music quickens to a rapturous movement and through the window alights the object of her dream —the spirit of the rose. With what joy, with what abandon does he dance—this being, blown hither and thither like a rose petal in the wind !

At his magic touch she is spirited out of her chair to join him in the ever-quickening soothing melody

of the waltz.   How high she leaps !   Yet so delicately
that it seems as if she, too, had forsaken her mortal
body.   Together they float through the still air,
impelled always by the fairy-like touch of his hand.
Slowly the music dies away—and ceases.   A moment,
and she is again in her chair ; her features calm in
repose, her dress unruffled, as if what had just tran-
spired was but an elfin touch of our imagination.
The rose-coloured sprite bends over her for a
brief instant, kisses her forehead, and in a flash
disappears through the open window just as the
first rays of dawn trace curious shadows upon the
wall.

The maiden stirs, smooths her sleep-laden eyes,
and looks around her as if questioning what was
only a dream were reality.   The room is empty !
Still doubting, she bends forward and retrieves her
precious rose.   Then she remembers.   Her face
lights up in a sad half-smile and she presses the
flower to her breast.

C. W. Beaumont.   *The Dancing World*.
December, 1922.

LEONID MASSINE IN " THE THREE-CORNERED HAT "

He slowly snaps his fingers and moves forward
with little, brisk steps—each advance punctuated by
a resounding thump of the feet.   Now he winds one
hand about the other while his feet crash to each
beat of the measure.   The pace quickens—he leaps
—revolves in mid-air—crashes to the ground with
another savage stamp of the feet.   He swings on one
foot alternately to right and left, then raises the free
foot to slap the heel sharply with the palm of each
open hand.   He whirls in a swift *pirouette*, falls to
the ground on his hands, and a second later leaps to
his feet.   The movement slows and he holds his
hands parallel to his chest, the palms facing, the
fingers slightly parted.   Now he turns slowly on
one foot and gradually raises and lowers his hands
with a plaintive fluttering of the fingers.   Again the

measure increases in speed—bursts into fiery rhythm. He moves with short, convulsive bounds —forward — backward — forward — backward—the street echoes to the swift chop of his feet as they continually strike the ground. One of his friends, with ever-quickening hand-claps, urges him to still greater efforts. So he leaps—faster—faster—the stamps grow louder—louder—the frenzy of rhythm quickens the pulse—fires the blood—a sudden deafening thud of the feet and the miller stops dead —quivering, breathless, streaked with sweat. *Ole ! Ole ! Bien Parado !*

C. W. Beaumont. *The Three-Cornered Hat.*

LEONID MASSINE AND LYDIA LOPOKOVA AS THE CAN-CAN DANCERS IN " LA BOUTIQUE FANTASQUE "

The shopkeeper . . . beckons to the porters, who wheel into the shop the low trolley upon which are posed a pair of Can-Can dancers. The man—the very symbol of the ill-famed *Salle Valentino*—is a dark, youthful rake, dapper to an exaggerated degree, in a tight-fitting cutaway coat and trousers of black velvet, check waistcoat, and patent shoes, while his crimped and curled glossy hair, pomaded side-whiskers, and curling moustache, would excite the envy of a barber's model. His companion is a lively little lady in a pale blue bodice and short white skirt, fringed with black lace, which ill conceals a wealth of lace petticoat, adorned with fetching bows of blue ribbon.

They slip to the floor and advance on one foot, the other raised in the air, twisting, turning, pointing to the lively air of the Can-Can. Now they separate, confront and retreat from each other. The man flaps his hands, throws back his head, falls forward on his toes, balances himself with a swift backward spring of his body. The lady alternately flings into the air each leg which writhes, twists, turns, revolves amid a foaming sea of lace and ribbon. They retreat, turn their backs on each other, and, while the lady flaunts her petticoats in mischievous abandon, the gentleman alternately posed on each foot, throws himself backwards with such verve that his body almost assumes the horizontal.

Now each extends a leg, and, supporting it with outstretched hand, they perform a dazzling series of *pirouettes*. Suddenly the gentleman falls to the floor and as the lady dances round continually whirling a leg over his head, he lowers his eyes and flaps his hands in mock horror at her naughtiness. He rises ; there is a brief repetition of the Can-Can, and the lady falls to the ground in a magnificent *écartement*. He quickly leaps to her side and as he whispers in her ear the figures become rigid and the performance ends.

C. W. Beaumont. *La Boutique Fantasque.*

ANNA PAVLOVA

Pavlova danced with her whole body, from the crown of her head to the tip of her toe. She danced with such abounding vitality, with such ecstasy of the spirit ; she surrendered herself so completely to the mood of the dance ; that she became a being transformed. She glowed, became almost incandescent, as it were, from the lavish outpouring of her nervous energy and muscular force. Sometimes there was just a pale luminosity which filled the spectator with an exquisite sadness as in *Le Cygne*, sometimes the glow burst into flame, as in *L'Autumne Bacchanale*. These two dances are poles apart and prove the immense scale of her accomplishment.

The fever which seized her in such moments of creation was instantly transmitted to the spectator. No sooner had she set foot on the stage than every member of the audience became aware of her presence. The whole atmosphere of the stage underwent a marked and subtle change ; there was a sense of tension, a kind of electrification of the air, a hint of marvels to come. Just as the microphone amplifies the slightest sound, so her least movement held the attention of the audience.

C. W. Beaumont. *Anna Pavlova.*

ANNA PAVLOVA : HER TECHNIQUE

Pavlova was best in *adage* and the dance *terre à terre*. Her *arabesques* and *attitudes* were poems expressed in line. Her movements *sur les pointes* reminded one of pearls strung on a silken thread, and in a *pizzicato* number her *pointes* rebounded from the ground " like golden arrows from a marble pavement," to borrow Gautier's picturesque phrase. She had a remarkable balance and could hold an *arabesque sur la pointe* for a quite unusual length of time. She turned *pirouettes* with an elegant ease, but though she rarely did more than two or three, she executed them with such a *brio* that they had the effect of half a dozen. She had a good *élévation*, as witness her *doubles cabrioles devant* in *Chopiniana*, but she rarely essayed the sustained and soaring flights associated with Taglioni, although she resembled her in the respect that she did not favour *temps de batterie.*

There was still another type of dance in which Pavlova excelled ; studies in *allégro* such as " *Papillons* " and " *La Libellule*, which positively sparkled owing to her incredibly quick darting movements, the brilliancy of her footwork, and the subtle and expressive play of her arms and hands.

C. W. Beaumont. *Anna Pavlova.*

VASLAV NIJINSKY AS HARLEQUIN IN " LE CARNAVAL "

Suddenly a slim, lithe, cat-like Harlequin took the stage. Although his face was hidden by a painted mask, the expression and beauty of his body made us all realise that we were in the presence of genius. An electric shock passed through the entire audience. Intoxicated, entranced, gasping for breath, we followed this superhuman being, the very spirit of Harlequin incarnate ; mischievous, lovable. The power, the featherweight lightness, the steel-like strength, the suppleness of his movements, the incredible gift of rising and remaining in the air and descending in twice as slow a time as it took to rise— contrary to all laws of gravitation—the execution of the most difficult *pirouettes* and *tours en l'air* with an amazing nonchalance and apparently no effort whatever, proved that this extraordinary phenomenon was the very soul of the dance.

Romola Nijinsky. *Nijinsky*.

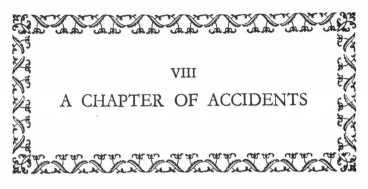

VIII

A CHAPTER OF ACCIDENTS

MADELEINE GUIMARD DISLOCATES HER ARM
(January, 1766)

Mlle. Guimard, while dancing to-day at the Opéra, was knocked down by a piece of scenery, which fell on her arm and dislocated it. Fortunately, Guerin, surgeon to the Musketeers, happened to be present, and he at once set the limb. It is to be hoped that there will be no disastrous after-effects. This young nymph bore the operation with great courage and did not utter a sound.

L. Petit de Bachaumont. *Mémoires Secrets.*

THE FIRE AT THE PARIS OPÉRA
(June 8th, 1781)

The act called *Coronis* concluded the performance and my father withdrew from it the more willingly in that he did not wish to break the charm of the music of *Orphée*. Towards the end of the ballet, which is very long in *Coronis*, Dauberval, one of the principal dancers, noticing that a cloth was burning, had the presence of mind to have the curtain lowered immediately, without waiting for the *divertissement* to end. The public thought the ballet somewhat short, but very fortunately made no comment on its abrupt conclusion. If they had uttered a protest it would have been made *en masse*. The spectators departed without alarm, hindrance, or disorder ; they ignored what was happening on the stage. The cloth that had caught fire was a border. A candle on a side-piece had set light to it. Water was at once called for, but none was available. There were shouts to cut the ropes which sustained the border, but this was done on one side only, the wrong side. The cloth, assuming a perpendicular position, gave added strength and fuel to the flame, which, running up the back-cloth, spread to the centre and then to all the borders with the utmost rapidity. As all efforts were without avail, the stage-hands and actors, witnesses of this scene of desolation, driven back by the smoke, sought safety in flight. The flames had already cut off the retreat of all those who were not on the stage.

The dancer Dangui, three tailors, and six stage-hands were burnt to ashes. Beaupré, brother of the well-known dancer, leaped from the third story and was killed ; one of his colleagues, taking the same course, broke his thigh. Huard, a tall, muscular dancer, having only two stories to clear, leaped towards the roof of a shop, slipped into the Cour des Fontanes and alighted on his feet without hurt. His servant, a boy of fifteen, remained at the window and feared to make the jump. Huard holds out his arms, calls to him, encourages him, saying that he is ready to catch him and break his fall. But nothing would induce the unfortunate boy to take the leap, not even the flames which soon reached him and burnt him alive before his master's eyes. Mlle. Guimard, fully undressed, without a chemise on her body, stifled and grilled in her dressing-room, and did not dare to move. A stage-hand ran to her assistance, wrapped her up in some curtains and carried her through the whirlwinds of smoke and flame.

Castil-Blaze.   *Histoire de l'Académie
Impériale de Musique.*

DIDELOT FALLS DURING A PERFORMANCE OF
NOVERRE'S BALLET, " L'AMOUR ET PSICHE "
(King's Theatre)

The very meritorious Didelot, Tuesday night, fell very violently, as he made his *entrée* in the concluding ballet ; he strained one of his ankles so much, that he was scarce able to walk off the stage : if he is able to dance again before May, it is as much as is expected.

Morning Herald, March 6th, 1788.

AUGUSTE VESTRIS FALLS THROUGH A TRAP

Vestris the dancer has had a very narrow escape for his life. This charming dancer, on Sunday the 11th instant, while performing at the Opera, experienced a fatal disaster ; on his alighting after a surprising vault, one of the traps gave way, and he fell seventeen feet and a half : fortunately a board, which accidentally lay across the machinery, stopped the further progress of the trap, or the fall would have been at least fifty feet. We are happy to add, he has received no other hurt, than what may be supposed from the shock !

Morning Herald, April, 1789.

MLLE. AUBRY FALLS FROM A GLOIRE IN " ULYSSE "
(February 27th, 1807)

This ballet, so admirably planned, ended in the greatest confusion ; a distressing accident turned the ending into a calamity. Minerva, who appears in a *gloire*, fell a distance of thirty feet, fractured her head, and almost broke a leg ; the part of Minerva was taken by Mlle. Aubry. It is impossible to convey the degree of consternation which this accident produced on all the actors and spectators ; on all sides women fainted ; nothing was heard but shouts of indignation and curses upon this criminal negligence and carelessness. Boutron, the former machinist, was in the theatre that very day, so it said, and, observing the faulty adjustment of the ropes of the *gloire*, prophesied disaster and foretold its fall. Boutron was Boulay's right hand ; a man skilled in the working of stage machinery and unusually precise and vigilant. Since he was dismissed from the Opera, I do not know on what grounds, all the artistes

who customarily sit in *gloires* have trembled for
their lives.

Journal de l'Empire, March 1st, 1807.

*

If one may credit the reports in the newspapers,
there is no need for anxiety regarding Mlle. Aubry's
condition.   A slight bruise on the forehead, such as
might be sustained by a child who fell over while
running ; a fractured arm ; a dislocated little toe of
the left foot or right ; a trifle hardly worth thinking
about.   It is none the less true that Mlle. Aubry's
plight is deplorable, she suffers the most acute pain ;
each day she develops some new trouble, which only
too frequently follows such great upsets ; and if she
saved her life she will lose an arm ; she will become
crippled and be deprived of the fruit of her talents
and of all hope of earning a livelihood.

Journal de l'Empire, March 10th, 1807.

A RARE ACCIDENT WITH AN UNUSUAL SEQUEL

Rey still reigned over the orchestra ... I remember
that one day Pouilly, who has since become a bass
at the Opéra, the great Pouilly, a dancer at that period,
taking part in a Warriors' Dance from *Trajan*, had
the misfortune to strike incorrectly the cymbals
which he played while dancing.   The precious
instrument broke, so that the cords alone remained
in the hands of the unfortunate cymbalist.   Rey, in
desperation at seeing the cymbals fly into pieces
towards the footlights, cymbals from Constantinople,
if you please, which the continental blockade had
made very rare and worth 1500 francs, Rey, furious,
put down his baton, stretched out his arms over the
fore-stage, picked up the pieces, and threw them
both forcibly and skilfully at the defenceless calves
of the unlucky cymbalist.   The musician in ambush,
attacking the dancer on the stage, was a redoubtable
foe, his cutting weapons would have inflicted painful
wounds.   So Pouilly forgot his part and asked the
Roman emperor for a respite, in order to attend to

his personal affairs. Unable to parry, he gave a leap every time a piece of bronze whistled through the air and menaced his calves, Pouilly was more skilful than Achilles, he evaded the blows and saved his tendons.

Castil-Blaze. *L'Académie Impériale de Musique.*

SHOCKING ACCIDENT TO A FRENCH DANCER

A French dancer, of the name of La Croix, who had come from St. Maloes to seek his fortune in Plymouth, finding the theatre there shut, and hearing of Monsieur Jefferson's company at Penzance, formed a resolution to pack up his very " little all," and *chassé* on foot to join them.

When he arrived at Penzance, he waited upon Mr. Jefferson, offered his services, and said, that he had no doubt he should draw crowded houses by the excellence of his performance ; for Monsieur La Croix, in his own opinion, was " *Le Dieu de la Danse.*" He was accordingly enrolled in the company on the usual terms, that is to say, that all should share and share alike. He made his appearance in a fine *pas seul,* but, unluckily, in one of his most graceful *pirouettes,* a very important part of his drapery, either from its age or slightness, or from the wonderful exertion of its wearer, became suddenly rent in a most unmendable manner. Shouts of laughter and applause followed, which Monsieur La Croix imagined were given for his jumping, nor was the supposition at all unjustifiable, for the higher he jumped, the more he was applauded. At last some one behind the scenes called him off the stage, and he was so shocked at the mishap which had befallen him, that he could never be induced to appear again.

Michael Kelly. *Reminiscences.*

MARIE TAGLIONI HAS A NARROW ESCAPE

The first performance of *Robert le Diable* was one succession of grave accidents, which might have had the most serious consequences. . . . After the beautiful periods of singing in the third act, after the chorus of demons, a cloth issued from below and ascended towards the " flies " by means of numerous wires ; many of these wires were carelessly attached, so that when the cloud cloth reached a certain height, quite close to the battens, it came undone and fell on the fore-stage ; Mlle. Taglioni, stretched out on her tomb, in the character of a statue not yet awakened to life, had only just time to resuscitate herself and leap aside to avoid serious injury.

Dr. L. Véron. *Mémories d'un Bourgeois de Paris.*

ACCIDENT TO TWO SYLPHIDES

At the performance given for Mlle. Taglioni's benefit, two sylphides remained suspended in mid-air, it was impossible to pull them up or lower them down ; people in the audience cried out in terror ; at last a machinist risked his life and descended from the roof at the end of a rope to set them free.   Some minutes later, Mlle. Taglioni, who only spoke this once in all her life (at the theatre, of course), went towards the footlights and said : " Gentlemen, no one has been hurt."

Théophile   Gautier.   *Histoire   de   l'Art Dramatique en France depuis Vingt-Cinq Ans.*

FANNY ELSSLER BRUISES HER FOOT IN " LA SYLPHIDE "

At the beginning of the ballet, there took place a little accident which, fortunately, had no serious consequences, but which at first alarmed us : at the moment when the Sylphide disappears through the fire-place (a strange exit for a sylphide) Mlle. Fanny Elssler, being carried too quickly by the counter-weight, knocked her foot violently against the frame of the chimney-piece.

Théophile   Gautier.   *Histoire   de   l'Art Dramatique en France depuis Vingt-Cinq Ans.*

PERILS OF THE DANCER'S PROFESSION

By dint of experiencing simulated danger, the

dancer becomes accustomed to real danger, just as the soldier, in war-time, becomes inured to murder and pillage. She is suspended by brass wire, she sits among cardboard clouds, she disappears through traps, she enters through fire-places, and she makes her exit through a window. In the first act of *La Péri* there is a leap so dangerous that I calculate that Carlotta Grisi risks her life each time she attempts it. Let M. Petipa be clumsy or merely distracted one evening and Carlotta will fracture her head on the stage. I know an Englishman who never misses a single performance of Théophile Gautier's piece. He is convinced that the ballet is destined to be fatal to Carlotta, and not for anything in the world would he be absent for a single evening.

Albéric Second. *Petits Mystères de l'Opéra.*

CARLOTTA GRISI INJURES HER FOOT

13, *Rue de Trevise,*
Monday.

Mlle. Carlotta Grisi presents her compliments to M. Cloquet. She begs that he will be so good as to take the trouble to come to 13, Rue de Trevise. If M. Cloquet cannot find time to do so, Mlle. Grisi will have herself taken to him. Eight days ago at the end of the performance of *Le Diable à Quatre*, Mlle. Grisi pricked her left heel with an enormous nail. The wound has healed up now, but the foot feels painful when placed on the ground.

CLARA WEBSTER'S SKIRT CATCHES FIRE

Last Saturday night a very lamentable accident took place at Drury Lane Theatre, during the performance of *The Revolt of the Harem*, which has proved fatal to Miss Clara Webster, the dancer. In the second act of the ballet, the ladies of the Harem are discovered bathing, among whom Zulica, the royal slave (Miss Webster), is one. During the scene, the gas placed at the bottom of the stage, or under the sunken portion of it, where the water pieces or waves, are placed, caught the light drapery of Miss Webster's dress, and in an instant her whole person was enveloped in flames.

This frightful event, taking place on the stage, in sight of the audience, the whole house was in a state of consternation, and screams issued from the ladies in front of the boxes and pit, who were the first to perceive the appalling accident.

The whole *corps de ballet*, who were on the stage with her, closed round her, to extinguish the flames, but, terrified at the appearance which presented itself, they retreated, and she rushed forward alone towards the front of the stage. Mrs. Plunkett alone endeavoured to extinguish the flames, and in so doing was herself nearly falling a victim to her intrepidity and good feelings. At this moment a carpenter belonging to the theatre sprang from the wing of the stage, and throwing himself upon the young lady, extinguished the fire by rolling upon her. In doing so, however, he severely cut her upper lip, and received some slight injury himself from the burning clothes. Miss Webster was immediately taken into the green-room, and placed upon a sofa. Her clothes were nearly all consumed, at least all her external garments. Fortunately, Dr. Marsden was in the theatre, and his assistance was rendered without delay. The usual applications of spirits of wine and water, flour, etc., were had recourse to, and every assistance was rendered. Miss Webster's face was much blistered, and in some parts scorched, the eyelashes and eyebrows burnt off ; but the hair of the head was untouched. The lower extremities were much scorched, and the flesh of the hips was also much burnt. The hands also suffered dreadfully. Miss Webster never lost her recollection, but exhibited, notwithstanding the dreadful agony under which she laboured, great physical power, and extraordinary moral fortitude.

The Illustrated London News, December 21, 1844.

ACCIDENT TO THREE WILIS IN "GISELLE"

The performance of the well-known ballet of *Giselle* produced at our Theatre Royal [Brussels] for the appearance of Mlle. Lucile Grahn, was interrupted a few evenings ago by an accident of a very serious nature. In the second act the Wilis have to appear through a trapdoor. Three *figurantes* were standing on the board under the stage ready to ascend, when the man whose duty it was to regulate the counter-weight let the rope slip from his hand. The consequence was that the unfortunate Wilis were drawn up with such velocity and force that, coming in contact with the trapdoor, which should have been opened, they forced it up. Several other *figurantes*, seeing what had happened, ran and extricated them. Two of the ladies were severely injured. One received a blow on the head which rendered her insensible and delirious ; and the arm of the other was much lacerated.

Cited under *Varietés Artistiques* in the *Programme of Her Majesty's Theatre*, February 23rd, 1847.

EMMA LIVRY'S SKIRT CATCHES FIRE

A most lamentable occurrence happened last Saturday [November 15th] at the Opéra. During a rehearsal of *La Muette* [*de Portici*] for Mario's *début*, Mlle. Livry was about to go on to the stage when all at once her skirt took fire from coming into contact with a gas-jet hanging from a piece of scenery, and the terrified young dancer crossed the stage with great bounds. It was a strange and affecting sight to see her walking amid fire. The fireman on duty seized Mlle. Livry, turned her upside-down, and stifled the flames. On seeing the dangerous plight of their friend, all the young members of the ballet went into hysterics. This emotion is explained by the interest taken in the graceful talent and virtuous and amiable character of Mlle. Livry.

First aid was rendered by Dr. Laborie and Dr.

Renegaud, who were present at the rehearsal. The burns, although superficial, are dangerous on account of their extent. Neither the neck nor the head was touched.

Le Constitutionel, November 17th, 1862.

MLLE. BARATTE'S SKIRT CATCHES FIRE

During a rehearsal of *Le Papillon*, Mlle. Baratte's skirt caught fire. M. de Saint-Georges dashed forward and was fortunate enough to smother the flame at the outset. The dancer escaped injury save for a few burns down her legs. None the less she danced at the first performance, but, in pulling off her tights, she took her skin off, too.

Anon. *Ces Demoiselles de l'Opéra*.

NICHOLAS LEGAT HAS FOUR TEETH KNOCKED OUT

I was dancing with the *ballerina* Olga Preobrazhenskaya at a charity performace at the Mihailoff Theatre. . . . We were doing my *Valse Caprice* to the music of Rubinstein, and I had just set my partner off in a spin of *pirouettes* when she accidentally raised her arm and caught me in the mouth with the full force of her elbow. I felt the blood spurt in my mouth with a horrible gush, but I had sufficient presence of mind to close my lips tightly and support my partner, so that she finished her brilliant movement in a graceful pose. In the enthusiasm of the moment she was quite unconscious of what she had done, and, as for me, I would rather have died than show it. So I finished the dance, including my solo, and managed to appear for two or three bows without anyone suspecting what had occurred. But when at the insistent applause Preobrazhenskaya pulled me by the arm and said : " We shall have to give an encore," I could hold out no longer. I was obliged to open my mouth and for answer spat four teeth out on the floor. Poor Olga swooned on the spot and was unable to continue the performance.

Nicholas Legat. *The Story of the Russian School.*
Trans. from the Russian by Sir Paul Dukes.

NICHOLAS LEGAT TEARS A TENDON

I was dancing with Claudia Kulichevskaya in *Pharaoh's Daughter*. The whole of the ballet went splendidly until the last act. Here, at the commencement of a *pas de deux* with my partner, all of a sudden I seemed to hear beneath my left foot a crunching sound. I thought I had trod on a nutshell or some other object dropped on the stage, and was about to step aside, when to my astonishment, I found the foot no longer responded. The foot gave way beneath me, and horrified to find myself a cripple, I hobbled off the stage on the other foot. It appeared that with the last movement of my solo I had torn a tendon in the ankle. . . . For three months I was on crutches, and was able to dance again only six months later.

Nicholas Legat. *The Story of the Russian School.*
Trans. from the Russian by Sir Paul Dukes.

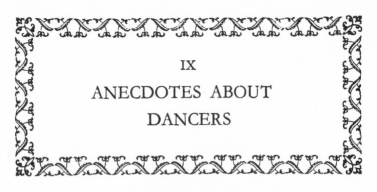

IX

ANECDOTES ABOUT DANCERS

PIGEONS AS AN AID TO CHOREGRAPHY

Beauchamps said that he had learned to compose the figures of his ballets from the pigeons in his loft. He took some corn with him and threw it to them. The pigeons ran to pick up the corn, and the different patterns and varied groups made by them inspired him with ideas for his dances.

François and Claude Parfait.
Histoire de l'Académie Royale de Musique.

CORELLI AND LECLAIR CHANGE PLACES TO THEIR MUTUAL ADVANTAGE

Two virtuosi were practising at the Rouen Theatre. One rehearsed leaps on the stage; the other, who played the violin in the orchestra, ordered the dancer's steps. The dancer, not at all pleased with the musician, said to him:

" The way you scrape your violin drives me mad."

" It may be," retorted the fiddler, " but you must admit that you dance like a lout. Why not become a musician as you have such a sensitive ear and so refined a taste, for cruel Nature has omitted to endow you with the agility and grace essential to a dancer ? "

" By the same token," replied the other, " why do you not learn to be a dancer ? The defects of your playing suggest that your talent may reside in your legs. Perhaps we have each taken the wrong road. Give me your violin—I already know the scales, and I will teach you to dance the minuets you make me play."

They were both right ; they changed places and

professions on the instant.   Both attained high rank
when they had taken the right path, and turned their
attention and efforts towards the new goal to which
their genius directed them.   Dupré was the dancer
escaped from the orchestra.   The ungraceful dancer,
a worthy rival of Corelli, was Leclair, who later
became our best violinist.

Castil-Blaze. *L'Académie Impériale de Musique.*

MARIE SALLÉ'S WORD

Passing through Paris, the illustrious Handel,
although always making fun of, and commenting
sarcastically upon, our French opera, appreciated the
talents of Mlle. Sallé.   A thousand crowns was the
sum she asked for composing two ballets and dancing
in them in London, during the Carnival of 1734.
The director of a rival enterprise having espied her
arrival in that city, made her an offer of three
thousand guineas in place of the three thousand
francs agreed upon with Handel, adding that there
was nothing to hinder her from making the change
because she had not yet signed the contract.

" And what about my word ! " said the amiable
dancer. " Does that count for nothing ? "

Castil-Blaze. *L'Académie Impériale de Musique.*

CAMARGO'S MELANCHOLY

Mlle. Camargo, so gay on the stage, was by nature
melancholy and serious ; and after having enraptured
the audience with joy and delight, and after having
obtained the greatest applause, her features took on
a tinge of sadness.   Hardly had she returned to the
wings than her charm disappeared and the pleasing
signs of delight and gaiety were effaced in an instant.

J. G. Noverre. *Lettres sur la
Danse, les Ballets et les Arts.*

AN UNWELCOME VISITOR AT A REHEARSAL

On the greensward of the park at Chantilly, lords
and ladies of the Court, dressed as woodland

creatures, fauns, and nymphs, rehearsed with the orchestra *Les Plaisirs de Diane*, a ballet which the Prince de Condé was preparing in honour of Louis XV. A tiger which had escaped from the menagerie, came and joined in the game. The nymphs took flight with appalling shrieks, the dryads fell into a swoon, the fauns and woodland creatures were not much braver. The ferocious animal, however, attacked no one, doubtless charmed by the music. When it had satisfied its curiosity, it allowed itself to be peacefully led back to its keepers.

Castil-Blaze. *L'Académie Impériale de Musique.*

GUIMARD'S ELIXIR OF YOUTH

Mlle. Guimard, like the Marshal de Richelieu, was a marvel ; ten years ago she had arrived at that fatal period when beauty must surrender its rights, and for ten years she had ceded nothing of her freshness and charm. Had time stood still for her ? No, but she made use of a practice then very much in vogue, but which she had brought to the height of perfection. When she was twenty years old, she caused her portrait to be painted by an able artist, then, with the aid of the likeness, she studied the different tones which made up her features, and when she had reduced the whole to a skilfully arranged set of colours, later on, each morning, without a single exception, Madeleine went to her dressing-room or rather her studio, then, placing a mirror at one side and her portrait at the other, she did not leave her boudoir until she had contrived an exact copy of the painting, so that at fifty she was a counterfeit of her appearance at twenty.

Castil-Blaze. *L'Académie Imperiale de Musique.*

GUIMARD'S BENEVOLENCE

It is said that Mlle. Guimard, the celebrated dancer of the Opéra, has just immortalised herself by an act of benevolence extraordinary. The Prince de Soubise being accustomed to give her every year some jewel as a New Year's gift, she asked him to make the gift a monetary one this year, giving him to understand that she was in need of it. Consequently this nobleman sent her the sum of 6,000 livres ; this was during the intense cold in January. Mlle. Guimard, furnished with this money, set out on foot alone, unattended by a single maid, and climbed all the third and fourth floors in her district, seeking out those who suffered from the severe weather and giving to each needy family something to feed, warm, and clothe themselves, and thus disbursed in a few days not only the whole of the 6,000 livres she had received, but also 2,000 livres of her own. It is said that all the facts are vouched for by the police ; because virtue loves to hide its good works, and we should never have made so honourable and touching a use of her New Year's gift. . . .

But I very much fear that Mlle. Guimard's fine action has not been reported correctly. All that I can discover for certain reduces itself to the fact that one day, her lackey not being at his post after the opera, she wished to reprimand him ; but he excused himself by saying that his mother was ill and in great distress on account of the cold. On hearing this the compassionate and tender Guimard ordered her lackey to take her to his mother, whom she tended with every care during her illness.

Grimm.   *Correspondance Littéraire*.

GUIMARD'S PHILOSOPHY

A nobleman once reproached her for opening her house so freely to all sorts of people.

" They will steal from you," he told her.

" It may be, I am resigned to it ; but you see, M. le Duc, if I should break my leg, or when I grow old, who knows but what I, too, shall have to knock at the doors of the Terpsichores of that day ! I give an example so that I may profit by it later."

Baronne d'Oberkirch.   *Mémoires*.

NOVERRE'S IRRITABILITY

Noverre produced his magnificent ballet of *" L'Iphigenie in Aulide "*; the splendour of the spectacle, the scenery, the richness of the decorations and dresses, could not have been surpassed; the dancing was of the first order, and the acting of D'Egville, in Agamemnon, inimitable; the triumphal cars, with horses, the grand marches, processions, and above all, the fine grouping of the *corps de ballet*, all was *vrai* classicality, and proved Noverre to be the greatest master of his art. But he was a passionate little fellow; he swore and tore behind the scenes, so that, at times, he might really have been taken for a lunatic escaped from his keeper.

I once felt the effects of his irritability. The horses attached to the car in which D'Egville was placed, were led by two men from Astley's, one of whom was so drunk that he could not go on the stage. I had been acting in the opera, but was so eager for the affray, and so anxious that things should go on right, that I had taken off my opera dress and put on that of a Grecian supernumerary, and with a vizor on my face, of course, was not known. I held one of the horses and all went correctly. I was standing behind the scenes, talking to one of the men, in my supernumerary dress, and perhaps rather loudly. Noverre, who was all fire and fury, came behind me and gave me a tremendous kick. *" Taisez-vous, bête,"* exclaimed he, and Noverre found that he had been kicking his manager; he made every possible apology, which I of course accepted, and laughed at the incident, at the same time begging him not to give me another such *striking* proof of his personal attention to the concern.

Michael Kelly. *Reminiscences.*

NOVERRE AND THE STATESMAN

Marie Antoinette, to whom he, Noverre, had given lessons, called him to Paris. Conscious of his standing as an artist, he knew how to maintain his prestige with dignity. A minister having sent for him, he excused himself on the grounds of business affairs and ill health, and only went at the third summons. The statesman did not conceal his displeasure. He expressed his surprise that a dancing-master should have to be asked three times before he came to see a minister. " I am not a stickler for titles," replied Noverre. "However, I must tell you that I am as much a dancing-master as Voltaire is a writing-master."

GAETANO VESTRIS AND THE CHACONNE

Vestris recently complained to him [Gluck] because the opera [*Iphigénie*] did not conclude with that dainty morsel known as a *Chaconne*, in which the dancer displays all his talents. M. Gluck, who treats his art with all the dignity it deserves, repeatedly told him that leaps and dances were out of place in so serious and lofty a theme. On his making renewed entreaties on behalf of his beloved *Chaconne*, the impatient composer replied :

" A *Chaconne* ! Would the Greeks, with whose customs we are dealing, have had them ? "

" They did not have them ! " exclaimed the astonished dancer. " Well, so much the worse for them."

Métra. *Correspondance Secrète*.

DR. JOHNSON DISCOURSES UPON DANCING

I ventured to mention a ludicrous paragraph in the newspapers, that Dr. Johnson was learning to dance of Vestris. Lord Charlemont, wishing to excite him to talk, proposed in a whisper, that he should be asked whether it was true. " Shall I ask him ? " said his lordship. We were, by a great majority, clear for the experiment. Upon which his Lordship very gravely, and with a courteous air, said : " Pray, sir, is it true that you are taking lessons of Vestris ? " This was risking a good deal, and required the boldness of a general of Irish

Volunteers to make the attempt. Johnson was at
first startled, and in some heat answered : " How can
your Lordship ask so simple a question ? "   But
immediately recovering himself, whether from un-
willingness to be deceived, or whether from real
good humour, he kept up the joke : " Nay, but if
anybody were to answer the paragraph, and con-
tradict it, I'd have a reply, and would say, that he
who contradicted it was no friend either to Vestris
or me.   For why should not Dr. Johnson add to his
other powers a little corporeal agility ? "

James Boswell. *Life of Johnson.*

AUGUSTE VESTRIS ON BEING SENT TO PRISON

The Count of Haga was the innocent cause of
a great event, the loss to the Opéra of the celebrated
Vestris.   Returned from London with a strained
foot, he could not dance on the day when the King
and Queen of Sweden were to have applauded him.
The Baron de Breteuil, the minister who had the
Opéra under his rule, sent Vestris to the prison of
La Force.

" It is the first time that our House has become
embroiled with the House of Bourbon," said that
little fop of a Vestris II.

Baronne d'Oberkirch. ˙ *Mémoires.*

AUGUSTE VESTRIS HAS HIS FOOT TRODDEN UPON

At this period [1778] he [Auguste Vestris] was
twenty-four and had been on the stage for four years.

A lady of my acquaintance told me this story ;
she had once encountered him in a crowd at the
Palais Royal.

" I unwittingly trod on his foot," said she, " without recognising him.   I turned round to make my
apologies, and enquired if I had hurt him.

" ' No, madam, but you have almost put all Paris
in mourning for a fortnight.'

" ' Ah ! ' cried my husband, ' it is Vestris.'

" ' You did not know me, sir,' he replied with a

disdainful look, ' but your wife knew quite well who I was.' "

Baronne d'Oberkirch. *Mémoires.*

AUGUSTE VESTRIS TURNS A PRETTY COMPLIMENT

At the ridotto ... when ... was present the beautiful Duchess of Devonshire, then in the full zenith of all her brilliance and attraction, the younger Vestris remarked to a bystander, in testimony of his profound admiration of her charms, that of all men living, he would choose to be the Duke of Devonshire were he not Vestris.

G. Yates. *The Ball ; or, A Glance at Almack's in* 1829.

STRANGE ORIGIN OF A FAMOUS BALLET

Dauberval, having occasion to satisfy a need of nature, stopped in front of a glazier's shop. He found his face pressed against a crude coloured print depicting a village youth fleeing from a cottage, with an angry old woman throwing his hat after him, while a peasant girl shed tears. At the end of a very short interval, the ravishing ballet *La Fille Mal Gardée* was evolved. How wonderful is genius !

Charles Maurice. *Histoire Anecdotique du Théâtre.*

DESPRÉAUX'S IMITATIONS OF DANCERS

Widowed for nine years from La Guimard, Despréaux has just died. I preferred his imitations of dancers to his writings, because they were amusing. Through the top of a tiny theatre, the curtain of which was half-lowered, he introduced on to the stage the first fingers of each hand, rigged out in a tunic, with tights and shoes fitted to the little legs. Then, to the strains of ballet music, he executed the *pas* so correctly that you could recognise the style and mannerisms of the dancer he wished to evoke.

Charles Maurice. *Histoire Anecdotique du Théâtre.*

DIDELOT WATCHES FROM THE WINGS

It was very amusing to see Didelot behind the scenes watching his pupils. Sometimes he swayed from side to side, smiled, and took mincing steps and stamped his foot. But when the little pupils danced he shook his fist at them, and if they missed the figures, he made their lives a misery. He pounced on them like a hawk, pulled their hair or ears, and, if any ran away, he gave them a kick which sent them flying. Even the solo dancers suffered from him. Being applauded, a dancer went behind the scenes, when Didelot seized her by the shoulders, shook her with all his might, and, having given her a punch in the back, pushed her on to the stage as if she were recalled.

A. Y. Golovacheva-Panaeva. *Memoirs.*

LA CANNE DE M. PIERRE GARDEL

Gardel, second of that name, died on the 9th of this month after having been *maître de ballet* at the Opéra for over fifty years. He was eighty-two (one year less than Vestris). He bequeathed to Albert the stick he used at rehearsals, a birthday present from Beaulieu. What in his hands amounted to a marshal's baton resembled neither Achilles' shield nor M. de Balzac's cane. It was a plain thorn stick with an ebony knob, on the top of which was Gardel's initial engraved on a mother-of-pearl shield.

Charles Maurice. *Histoire Anecdotique du Théâtre.*

THE OMNIPOTENT PIERRE GARDEL

Never did manager or author enjoy such respect from their subordinates as the Gardel of our day. There were times when this famous *maître de ballet* never attended a rehearsal but what he was dressed entirely in black with powdered hair, and with a sword at his side. At his approach the artistes and students formed a lane down which the choregrapher-teacher passed like a king followed by his retinue.

Charles Maurice. *Histoire Anecdotique du Théâtre.*

LORD FIFE AND MLLE. NOBLET

Among our countrymen who had the *entrée* to the *foyer* or greenroom, Lord Fife made himself the most conspicuous by his unremitting attentions to Mlle. Noblet, whom he never quitted for an instant. He would carry her shawl, hold her fan, run after her with her scent-bottle in his hand, admire the diamond necklace some one else had given her, or gaze in ecstasy on her *pirouettes.*   On his return to London, the old *roué* would amuse George IV with a minute description of the lady's legs, and her skill in using them.

Capt. Gronow. *Reminiscences and Recollections.*

A SLIP OF THE TONGUE

One of our countrymen having been introduced by M. de la Rochefoucauld to Mademoiselle Bigottini, the beautiful and graceful dancer, in the course of conversation with this gentleman, asked him in what part of the theatre he was placed, upon which he replied : " Mademoiselle, *dans une loge rôtie,*" instead of " *grillée.*"   The lady could not understand what he meant, until his introducer explained the mistake, observing : " *Ces diables d'Anglais pensent toujours à leur rosbif.*"

Capt. Gronow. *Reminiscences and Recollections.*

MERCANDOTTI'S ELOPEMENT

Among the number of hearts on whom the bewitching eyes of the beautiful Spaniard made an impression, was that of a gentleman well known as a man of wealth and fashion, Mr. Hughes Ball.

On the 16th March, I received a note in the following words :

H

16 Mars, 1823

Monsieur,

Ma santé étant extrêmement dérangée, j'ai consulté mon médecin, qui m'a conseillé d'aller à la campagne pour passer quelque temps ; je m'empresse de vous en prévenir, afin que vous puissiez donner mon rôle à une autre personne.

J'ai l'honneur d'être,
Monsieur,
Maria Mercandotti.

It was soon made public that Mercandotti had a more agreeable cause of absence than ill-health, and that she had accepted the hand offered to her at length by Mr. Ball.

The papers were, as usual, prompt in taking up the subject of the elopement, and epigrams and *jeux d'esprit* without number appeared at the time. One was a version of her note to me, and ran as follows :

" Sir, being a-miss et ma santé dérangée,
  Mon médicin declares qu'il-y-a quelque chose à
      changer ;
  I suppose he means air—à la campagne je vais,
  So dispose of my rôle à quelque autre, I pray.
  But Mamma ne veut pas que je suis paresseuse,
  Bids me go to a Ball, and I cannot ref-Hughes."

Again :

" Mercandotti's gone ; well, where is the wonder,
    And why should we wish her last step to recall ?
  The light-footed nymph has committed no blunder,
    The Dancer has only gone off with the Ball."

John Ebers. *Seven Years of the King's Theatre.*

" LES RATS DE L'OPÉRA "

General D——, a fine old veteran of the Empire, and an *habitué* of the *coulisses* at the time I speak of [1815], asked me a few years since to accompany him to the Opéra, which, from a prolonged absence from Paris, he had not visited for many years. When we arrived, after taking a good survey with his glass, he observed : " I find they now call the young ladies we used to call *figurantes, des rats de l'opéra.* I am curious to see them again." At this moment a whole army of young sylphides, more o less pretty, came fluttering across the stage. My friend looked at them attentively with his lorgnette, and at last exclaimed with a sigh : " *Mais je ne reconnais plus ces rats là.*" " *Je crois bien, mon Général,*" said I, " *les vôtres n'auraient plus de dents pour grignotter leur prochain.*"

Capt. Gronow.   *Reminiscences and Recollections.*

MARIE TAGLIONI'S PHYSIQUE

Her legs recalled those of Diana, her chest was short and narrow, her arms were very long. Taglioni's father, who produced a great many ballets abroad, had, before leaving, entrusted his daughter, still quite young, to M. Coulon. This professor of dancing then enjoyed a great reputation. Poor Marie Taglioni became the butt for the mockery of her companions. " Will that little hunchback," said one, " ever learn to dance ? "

Dr. L. Véron.   *Mémoires d'un Bourgeois de Paris.*

MARIE TAGLIONI'S FIRST VISIT TO THE THEATRE SCHOOL, ST. PETERSBURG

(September, 1837)

The most celebrated dancer Taglioni arrived at St. Petersburg with her father and came to our school to do her exercises. The director and the officials treated her with every courtesy. Taglioni was a very plain, excessively thin woman with a small, yellowish, and very wrinkled face. I felt quite ashamed because after the class the pupils surrounded Taglioni, and, with a charming note in their voices, said in Russian : " What an ugly mug you've got ! How wrinkled you are ! " Taglioni, not knowing the language and thinking compliments

were being paid to her, smiled and replied in French :
" Thank you, dear children."

A. Y. Golovacheva-Panaeva. *Memoirs.*

MARIE TAGLIONI'S RESOURCE

On arrival at the pretty town of Perth, in the
Highlands, she was given the visitors' book in
which she inscribed her name, her real name.
What a blunder ! What an insult for the pretty
town ! To imagine that the name of Taglioni had
not been heard of there ! Mistakes never come
singly, her plaid became disarranged, a feather fell
from her wings, and that feather was not lost.

After having taken a walk on the banks of the Tay,
the sylphide returned to dine ; a deputation from
the nobility and gentry of the pretty town and its
suburbs waited on her. This deputation entreated
her to accord them a performance of *Nathalie*, her
last creation at London, just one performance only.
All the guineas in that pretty little town awaited but
the signal to pass into her handbag. The great
dancer allowed herself to be won over, and they
took advantage of her weakness. But what a
theatre ! What a company ! What scenery ! To
perform a ballet there were only lacking a *corps
de ballet*, a male partner, and scenery. Eh ! what
mattered a male partner more or less, a *corps de
ballet* more or less, scenery more or less improvised ?
What every one wished to see, admire, and applaud
was the great dancer—Taglioni.

During the first act, although the most difficult
one, the ballet did not falter, but when it came to the
second it seemed as though all must be ruined.
You know, or do not know, that in the second act
the lover takes the place of a dummy on which the
stupid Nathalie lavishes a thousand foolish en-
dearments.

But when the curtain was about to be raised, it
was found that the dummy had been forgotten !
Oh, father Taglioni, for much less Vatel, the innocent

Vatel had transfixed himself with his sword. Mlle.
Taglioni does not lose her head.

" Pierre," she quickly says to her valet, " you will
act the dummy " . . . and she goes on the stage.

Pierre, rigged out grotesquely, is in turn about to
go on the stage.

" Wait ! " the manager suddenly cries. " Wait ! He
has whiskers which the lover has not ; no one would
take him for the other. Hey ! barber, come here and
shave off his whiskers."

The dummy refuses to be shaved, he is fond of
his whiskers. The manager insists ; Pierre becomes
angry. The manager was diplomatic and con-
ciliating, he made a signal and Pierre was seized,
clapped into a chair, held down and shaved.

Meanwhile the time slipped on. Already the
dummy was several minutes overdue at his post,
the action began to falter ; but when Taglioni is on
the stage, how can the action falter ? That evening
Taglioni improvised for the pretty town adorable,
captivating steps such as she had never danced either
at London or at Paris ; she had imagined everything,
forseen all. From time to time she approached the
wings :

" Is he ready ? " she asked.

" A few more *entrechats*," was the reply, and she
again leaped in the most charming manner.

At last the shaven dummy appeared and the
public, who suspected nothing, almost took it in
bad part that he made his entrance too soon.

Charles de Boigne. *Petits Mémoires de l'Opéra.*

MARIE TAGLIONI PAID ONE HUNDRED POUNDS A PERFORMANCE
(1836)

One of the principal objects I had in view in
coming on this occasion to Paris, was to effect an
engagement with Mademoiselle Taglioni. . . .

The only drawback to my enthusiasm on the
present occasion was that I had to pay such an

enormous price for indulging in it, being unable to effect an engagement with this " Spirit of Air " on any other terms than 100*l.* per night for herself, 600*l.* for the term of her visit to her father as ballet-master, 900*l.* to her brother and sister-in-law to dance with her, two benefits guaranteed to produce her 1,000*l.*, and half a benefit guaranteed to produce her brother 200*l.*, involving altogether a sum of more than 6,000*l.*

Alfred Bunn. *The Stage.*

MARIE TAGLIONI RENEWS ACQUAINTANCE WITH HER HUSBAND

It was in 1852 when I saw Taglioni again, at the Comte de Morny's house, some days after his resignation as Minister of the Interior. He had invited some of his artist friends to dinner. Although it was confined to men, he had two ladies sitting beside him, Mlle. Taglioni and Mlle. Rachel. They might have been two ladies of title, so carefully did they observe the simplicity which distinguishes the best style. I was sitting between Delacroix and the Comte Gilbert de Voisins, who arrived when the guests were already at table. His first words were :

" Who is that schoolmistress on Morny's right ? "

I did not think he would be very upset when I said to him :

" It is your wife."

He searched his memory for a long time before replying :

" Ah, well, it may be so."

Mlle. Taglioni, indicating her husband, asked Morny why he had had the extraordinary idea to ask her to dine in such bad company.

When dinner was over, Gilbert de Voisins, who feared nobody, not even his wife, had the impertinence to ask to be introduced to her. She took the pleasantry well.

" It seems to me, sir," said she, " that I already

had the honour of making your acquaintance about 1832."

That was the fatal year of their marriage. The day after the wedding, Gilbert de Voisins had forgotten that he was married.

Arsène Houssaye. Les Confessions.

THE LIGHTNESS OF GRISI AND PERROT

The Zephyr has a sister, mythologically speaking. Perrot has required all his elasticity to follow Carlotta in her flight. Who is the lighter of the two ? When they are in the air they do not fall, they descend ; no one throws them flowers, they show them bouquets from the boxes, then they rise and take them : that is all there is to it.

Jacques Arago. Physiologie des Foyers.

AMALIA FERRARIS AT HOME

Amalia Ferraris was a dancer at the theatre only.

In town, in her little flat in the Rue de Provence or the Rue de la Victoire—I forget which—it was difficult to get her away from her *polenta*, her *rizotto*, her *ravioli*—and her husband.

Anon. Ces Demoiselles de l'Opéra.

PAULINE DUVERNAY AND THE POWER OF TEARS

This young dancer, brought up by a clever mother, had made a particular study of the power of tears. One day, when she was to dance a *pas* with Mlle. Lise Noblet, I went to see her, and found her sobbing ; I enquired the reason for such profound grief ; my alarmed curiosity was received with the most obstinate silence. Her mother, a witness of my entreaties, laughingly reassured me. " I will tell you everything, she dances this evening with Mlle. Noblet ; Mlle. Noblet has very beautiful jewels, my daughter has none." Despite my long experience, a woman's tears always affect me, and I at once sent to Mme. Janisset for the sovereign remedy against such great sufferings and such poignant sorrow. It was one of my days of managerial weakness.

Dr. L. Véron. *Mémoires d'un Bourgeois de Paris.*

MORE ABOUT DUVERNAY'S TEARS

Mlle. Leroux was always laughing, Mlle. Duvernay was often in tears. Vestris, distressed at her sadness and to arouse my sympathy, would point to the floor bedewed with drops from the watering-can. " Look ! " he said to me, " there are her tears ! " Behind the scenes, even in the morning, before they were dressed up, every one acted.

Dr. L. Véron. *Mémoires d'un Bourgeois de Paris.*

PAULINE DUVERNAY RECEIVES A LESSON

The mother of the dancer, Mlle. Duvernay, did not fail to be exacting on her daughter's behalf, and, while asking me for a seat in the stalls for the evening performance, remarked in a pompous tone : " My daughter's talent has no need of any one's influence." I made no reply until the evening performance, when I instructed the chief of the *claque* that his men were not to accord Mlle. Duvernay a single hand-clap. Counting on the customary flourish of applause from the *claque*, Mlle. Duvernay, on finishing her *pirouette*, smiled graciously at the audience and seemed to offer thanks in advance for the expected applause ; but the theatre maintained the deepest silence, to the astonishment and disappointment of the young dancer, and to the fury of her mother, who considered herself insulted. " One swallow does not make a summer," I told her, " but you must see that your daughter's talent does need some help."

Dr. L. Véron. *Mémoires d'un Bourgeois de Paris.*

DUVERNAY AND THE POWER OF LOVE

A young secretary at the Embassy, poor as Job, also sighed for Miranda.[1]

[1] Miranda is the principal role in the opera-ballet *La Tentation* and was taken by Pauline Duvernay.

" It is not money that I would offer you," he cried (he had good reason to say so) : it is my life, my life that I would be happy to sacrifice for you."

" If I asked you for your head, you would bring it to-morrow, wouldn't you ? " she said, laughing. " Ah, you men, you're all alike ; you always offer what one cannot, or does not, wish to take."

" I swear to you——"

" Don't swear, I will take you at your word.

" Good Heavens ! What do I hear ! Speak, I beg of you."

" Do you wish me to ? "

" I implore you to."

" Very well, make me a present of one of your teeth : that one in the middle."

" I run, I fly—I will return ! "

He had already vanished.

Mlle. Duvernay found that the diplomat did not come off badly in the tooth test. An hour had barely passed when the diplomat reappeared : in one hand he held a handkerchief pressed to his mouth, in the other he held out a pill-box. It contained the desired tooth ; she opens the box and at the same instant he opens his jaws, showing the gap in his teeth made by the dentist's forceps.

" But, how stupid ! " cried Miranda. " I asked you for the bottom tooth and you have brought me the top one ! "

Charles de Boigne.   *Petits Mémoires de l'Opéra.*

DUVERNAY AS A MIME

In *La Révolte au Sérail*, during the military manœuvres of the *corps de ballet*, the superior officers of the army form a council of war on the stage ; the theme stated nothing more ; but when Mlle. Duvernay was given one of the principal parts, she endeavoured, by means of the wittiest miming and the most expressive and most passionate gestures, to express all the phases of a most animated discussion, and to give an idea of a council of war held by women.   Universal laughter and applause greeted these gay and comical scenes.

Dr. L. Véron.   *Mémoires d'un Bourgeois de Paris.*

VÉRON'S METHOD OF DOING BUSINESS

The most perfect managerial adept I ever met is my friend *Monsieur* Véron, who, at the time he was *directeur* of the Académie Royale de Musique at Paris, visited this country for the purpose of engaging *Les Demoiselles Elssler.* He gave them a splendid dinner at the Clarendon, and when the dessert was put upon the table, the centre piece was a large salver of *bijouterie* for each of them to select one trinket from, of a given value, in addition to the theatrical engagement he offered them.   It was not only an elegant but a very politic mode of arranging business ; for while they would have otherwise have been disputing half the time upon a question of a few hundred francs, a bauble, of not half the value, decided it at once.

Alfred Bunn.   *The Stage.*

HOW OLD DUMILÂTRE HELPED HIS DAUGHTERS

This worthy retired tragedian spent his leisure hours in applauding his two daughters, Mlles. Sophie and Adèle Dumilâtre.   In common fairness, I must say that he carried out this perilous task with a tact, a grace, and a delicacy beyond all praise.

" Ah, sir," said he, to his neighbour, " who is that charming young lady ? "

" That is Mlle. Adèle Dumilâtre."

" I am much obliged to you, sir.   How pretty she is !   How pretty she is !   Ah, really, no one could be prettier than she is ! "

Enter Sophie Dumilâtre—same question from old Dumilâtre, same answer from the obliging neighbour.

" Ah, sir.   I am much obliged to you.   How she dances !   How she dances !   Ah, really, no one could dance like she does ! "

But one day, so I was told, the neighbour happened

to be a follower of the drama who remembered
Arbute, Arcas, Théramène, and other tragic parts.

" By Jove, old Dumilâtre," said he, " you ought to
know those girls—they are your own daughters ! "

Albéric Second. *Petits Mystères de l'Opéra.*

CUPID GOES TO MARKET

The day after her [Mlle. Eugénie Fiocre's]
appearance in the ballet *Pierre de Medicis*, in which
she took the part of Cupid, to the great satisfaction
of the gentlemen in the stalls, I met her in walking
dress, in the Boulevard Bonne Nouvelle, carrying
under her arm a basket from which protruded a
bundle of carrots and a parcel of leeks. " What !
Cupid going to market ! " I cried involuntarily, and
the poor child blushed at my remark, doubtless
under the impression that I intended a witticism
at her expense, where I saw merely an antithesis
in action.

Nerée Desarbres. *Sept Ans à l'Opéra.*

THE DIPLOMACY OF LUCILE GRAHN

What a woman she is, sir, that fair daughter from
the North ! Despite her fragile appearance, Lucile
Grahn has the strength and figure to stir a whole
world. She possesses diplomatic genius in its most
subtle, most intangible, and most ethereal from.
She is a Metterneich added to a Talleyrand. She
is the whole Congress of Vienna in petticoats.

The story of her first appearances at the Opéra,
six years ago, deserves to be celebrated in hexameters.
Alone, unaided, hardly able to speak our tongue,
endowed with a talent then distinctly questionable,
and with a spotless virtue, Lucile Grahn found the
way to shake the earth and turn heaven upside-down.
Every day, at seven in the morning, whatever the
weather, she set out on foot to survey Paris from
end to end, distributing on her way the most gracious
looks and the sweetest smiles.

Albéric Second. *Petits Mystères de l'Opéra.*

HOW FANNY CERRITO IMPROVED HER FEATURES

Cerrito, when a young girl, had a heavy cast of face redeemed by beautiful blue eyes.   In all her spare moments she used to look at herself in a pocket-mirror she always carried, and, by dint of constantly working her features and massaging her face, in course of time she contrived to fashion herself a charming countenance.

Extracted from a Commonplace Book.

FANNY CERRITO'S FATHER

Cerrito possessed, perhaps still possesses, a father; an old boy as tender as he was devoted.   Nothing can compare with the admiration he felt for his daughter.   He never referred to her except as *La Divinita*.   There are two fathers in M. Cerrito, the London papa and the Paris papa.   At London, he has his pockets full of the *Divinita's* old ballet shoes, garlands which have been thrown to her, declarations of love sent her by all the princes in Europe, and contracts at fabulous sums which she has scorned; he produces them, displays them, renders them all honour and glory; he never goes out for a walk without being attended by half a dozen bodyguards, hired Italian applauders attached to his person.

Charles de Boigne.   *Petit Mémoires de l'Opéra.*

THE JUDGMENT OF SOLOMON

With such materials in my grasp as the four celebrated *danseuses*, Taglioni, Carlotta Grisi, Cerito, and Lucille Grahn, it was my ambition to unite them all in one striking *divertissement*. . . .

All was at length adjusted.   Satisfaction was in every mind; the *pas de quatre* was rehearsed—was announced; the very morning of the event had arrived; no further hindrances were expected. Suddenly, while I was engaged with lawyers in my own room, deeply occupied with the final arrangements for my purchase of the opera-house (of which more hereafter), poor Perrot rushed unannounced into my presence in a state of intense despair. Without regard for the serious conclave assembled, he uttered frantic exclamations, tore his hair, and at last found breath to say that all was over—that the *pas de quatre* had fallen to the ground and never could be given. With difficulty the unfortunate ballet-master was calmed down to a sufficient state of reason to be able to explain the cause of his anguish. The completion of the purchase of the opera-house was suspended for a few minutes and the explanation came, as follows :

When all was ready I had desired Perrot to regulate the order in which the separate *pas* of each *danseuse* should come. The place of honour, the last in such cases (as in regal processions), had been ceded with out over-much hesitation to Mademoiselle. Of the remaining ladies who claimed equal rights, founded on talent and popularity, neither would appear before the other. " *Mon Dieu !* " exclaimed the ballet-master in distress, " *Cerito ne veut pas commencer avant Carlotta—ni Carlotta avant Cerito, et il n'y a pas moyen de les faire bouger ; tout est fini.*"

" The solution is easy," said I to poor Perrot. " The question of talent must be decided by the public. But in this dilemma there is one point on which I am sure the ladies will be frank. Let the oldest take her unquestionable right to the envied position."

The ballet-master smote his forehead, smiled assent, and bounded from the room upon the stage. The judgment of the manager was announced. The ladies tittered, laughed, drew back, and were now as much disinclined to accept the right of position as they had been before eager to claim it. The ruse succeeded. The management of the affair was left in Monsieur Perrot's hands. The order of the ladies being settled, the *grand pas de quatre* was finally performed on the same night before a de-lighted audience, who little knew how nearly they had been deprived of their expected treat.

Benjamin Lumley. *Reminiscences of the Opera.*

PERROT COMPOSES A BALLABILE

When the moment of inspiration seized him, he squatted on the stage, his head between his hands. He might have been a china monkey. When the *corps de ballet* saw him seated on the ground like a tailor, they knew it would be for a long time, and so every one made themselves comfortable accordingly ; some embroidered, some lunched, some read, the solo dancers had refreshments brought to them. After a long interval a certain noise was heard. It was Perrot snoring. He was awakened ; the *ballabile* was finished ; it had arrived with the snoring.

Charles le Boigne. *Petits Mémoires de l'Opéra.*

STRANGE COINCIDENCE

When M. Feydeau began to write *Monsieur de Saint-Bertrand*, he asked Mlle. Emma Livry to explain to him certain dance terms of whose meaning he was ignorant.

Emma Livry did more, she danced for the novelist's particular benefit the very *pas* from *La Sylphide* which he wished to describe.

Some days later he went to thank her.

" At least," said she, " tell me the story of your novel."

M. Feydeau told her the story of *Le Mari de la Danseuse*.

When he had concluded, Emma Livry became thoughtful, then, turning to her mother, she said :

" To be burnt to death, that must be very painful ! "

Then, a moment later :

" All the same, it is a fine death for a dancer."

Anon. *Ces Demoiselles de l'Opéra.*

BEAUGRAND'S FIRST SIGHT OF THE OPÉRA

When a very thin child she descended from the heights of La Villette to join the *petite classe* in the Rue Richer where poor little things were brought up by being made to work. It was extraordinary the way she entered the Opéra. One night a dancer was

needed to take the part of a page in a forgotten ballet
called *Jovita*.   Someone went to the *petite classe* in
the Rue Richer.   But there was only a skinny child
tiring herself in exercising her limbs.   The *maître
de ballet* made a face on seeing her, he wanted a
pretty girl, pretty in the accepted sense of the word,
because Mlle. Beaugrand, who is not at all pretty, is
worse, as Mme. Dorval said.   But, having no choice,
he took Beaugrand.

Come to the Opéra !

To the Opéra !   She !   Can you imagine the
feverish excitement of that child who had never seen
the Opéra and who was being taken there, to that
immense building that she believed to be all golden
like a palace and as holy as a temple.   She trembled
on arriving there.   She was taken to the dresser.   The
maître de ballet grimaced.   The dresser pouted.

What !   Is she going to replace the page ?   That
little sixpen'orth of ha'pence !

Poor Beaugrand almost wept !   But she was at the
Opéra, treading its sacred boards, she saw the public
opposite her.   And, moreover, she had come into a
fortune—tenpence a day !   How welcome those
pennies were in that little shop in La Villette !

Anon. *La Vie à Paris.*

THE STERN CALL OF DUTY

One night a dancer's mother, sobbing, entered
her daughter's dressing-room just as she had completed her make-up.

" Oh, my child, your poor father is dead ! "

The daughter dabbed her eyes with a handkerchief,
then, stifling a sob, she said :

" Oh, mother, why did you tell me this now ?   How
can I cry ?   It would ruin my make-up."

Anon. *Ces Demoiselles de l'Opéra.*   1885.

THE CORPS DE BALLET SEE THE BRETON CAPS THEY ARE
TO WEAR IN " LA KORRIGANE "

Accustomed to represent flowers, butterflies, or
stars, they could not bring themselves to put the

Breton caps on their heads, notwithstanding their prettiness and diversity. " We shall look like servants," they said, in indignation. Some even dissolved in tears.

These tears were soon dried by the happy result of the first performance. . . . The success was triumphal and to-day *La Korrigane*, which has hardly left the bill, nears its one hundredth performance, a rare fortune for a ballet.

> François Coppée. *A propos d'un Ballet*
> (*Figaro Illustré*, February, 1895).

MATILDA KSHESSINSKAYA'S WILL POWER

Matilda timed her reappearances to the height of the season, allowing herself long intervals, during which she left off regular practice.   In her holidays, she became untiring in the pursuit of pleasure. Fond of parties, cards, ever laughing, amazingly bright ; late hours never impaired either her looks or her temper.   She possessed a marvellous vitality and a quite exceptional will-power.   Within a month preceding her appearance, she completely subordinated her life to her work.   She trained for hours, ceased to receive and go out, went to bed at ten, weighed herself every morning, always ready to restrict further her already frugal diet.   Before the performance she stayed in bed twenty-four hours, taking only a light meal at noon.   At six o'clock she was at the theatre, allowing herself two full hours in which to make up and practise.   One evening I happened to be practising on the stage at the same time as her ; I noticed a feverish glitter in her eyes.   " Oh ! " she said, in answer to my enquiry, " I have been simply dying for a drop of water the whole day, but I won't drink before dancing."

> Thamar Karsavina. *Theatre Street.*

NIJINSKY'S COSTUME IN " LE SPECTRE DE LA ROSE "

Bakst's original design for the costume was done

on Nijinsky himself. He sketched it on the shirt Nijinsky was wearing. Bakst had painted samples of silk pongee, in rose, rose-lavender, dark reds, and various pinks, and these were given to Maria Stepanovna to have bolts of the material dyed. Bakst cut the forms of the rose-petals himself. Some had to be tight, others loose, and he instructed her just how to sew them on so that the costume was created anew each time Nijinsky danced. It consisted of a close-fitting, fine, silk elastic jersey, into which Nijinsky was sewn, covering his entire body, except part of his breast and arms, where bracelets of silk rose-petals bound his biceps. This jersey was stitched with rose-leaves, which Bakst would colour as they were needed. Some were ragged, as from a dying flower ; others were stiff and firm ; while still others curled even from his thighs. And after every performance Maria Stepanovna would refresh them with her curling-iron. On his head he wore a close-fitting helmet of rose-leaves, and the whole effect was an extremely close blending of different reds, rose-violet, pink, and purple, shading one into another, which is the essential indefinable tint of the rose.

Nijinsky's make-up was conceived to personify a rose. His face was like that of a celestial insect, his eyebrows suggesting some beautiful beetle which one might expect to find closest to the heart of a rose, and his mouth was like rose-petals.

Romola Nijinsky. *Nijinsky.*

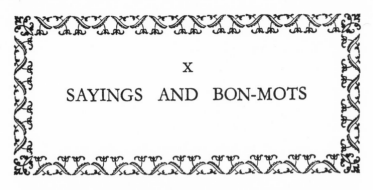

X
SAYINGS AND BON-MOTS

PÉCOURT'S RETORT TO THE MARSHAL DE CHOISEUL

The Marshal de Choiseul, meeting the famous Pécourt at the house of Ninon, of whom they were both lovers, and seeing the dancer dressed in a suit cut in the style of the uniforms of the period, chaffed him thus :

"Ah! Ah! How long have you been a soldier, M. Pécourt, and in what corps do you serve?"

"Marshal," retorted the spiteful dancer, "I command a corps in which you have long served."

Castil-Blaze. *L'Académie Impériale de Musique.*

PLUS ÇA CHANGE—

Arethuse, an opera-ballet by Danchet and Campra, produced February 24th, 1735, having received a lukewarm reception, means were discussed for improving its chances of success.

"I can think of one way only," said Campra, "and that is to lengthen the dances and shorten the dancers' skirts."

Castil-Blaze. *L'Académie Impériale de Musique.*

A PUNNING EPITAPH

Mlle. Du Miré, of the Opéra, more celebrated as a courtesan than as a fine dancer, has just buried her lover. Parisian wits, who see fun in everything, have contrived the following epitaph, to be carved in music characters on his tombstone :

Mi Ré La Mi La.[1]

L. Petit de Bachaumont. *Mémoires Secrets.*

---

[1] Pun on the phrase : *Miré l'a mis là*, that is, Miré put him there.

SOPHIE ARNOULD ON MADELEINE GUIMARD

I cannot understand why that little silk-worm is not fatter—it lives on such a nice leaf.

(A double allusion to Guimard's extreme thinness and to the wealth lavished upon her by her protector, Monseigneur Louis S. de Jarente de la Bruyère, Bishop of Orleans.)

GAETANO VESTRIS ON HIS SON, AUGUSTE

Auguste is more skilful than I, the explanation is simple ; Gaetano Vestris is his father ; an advantage which Nature has denied me.

AUGUSTE VESTRIS ON HIMSELF

In Europe there are only three great men—myself, Voltaire, and the King of Prussia.

GAETANO VESTRIS'S LITTLE QUIP

At the son's [Auguste Vestris] benefit yesterday George S—n, in order to humour French variety, advised the father [Gaetano Vestris] it was the *first day* he had ever seen so many people gathered together. " And it will be *the last day*," returned the king of capers, " before you will see so many gathered together again."

The Morning Chronicle. February 24th, 1781.

FREDERICK THE GREAT AND NOVERRE

After the play the Emperor said to the King of Prussia : " There is Noverre, the famous chore-grapher ; I think he used to be at Berlin." Noverre made him a beautiful dancing-master's bow. " Ah, I know him," said the King, " we saw him at Berlin —he was very amusing ; he could mimic any one, especially our *danseuses*, till you died of laughter." Noverre, not very pleased at this way of being remembered, made another beautiful bow in the third position, and expressed the hope that the King would afford him some small opportunity for revenge. " Your ballets are beautiful," said the King, " your *danseuses* are graceful, but their grace is somewhat artificial. I think you make them raise their arms and shoulders too much; for if you remember, our *première danseuse* at Berlin was not like that." "That was why she was at Berlin, Your Majesty," retorted Noverre.

Letter of the Prince de Ligne to the King of Poland (1785).

NAPOLEON I AND MLLE. BIGOTTINI

One day when her [Bigottini's] dancing had given particular pleasure to the Emperor, he commanded Fontanes to send her a token of his appreciation.

Fontanes could think of nothing better than to send the dancer a whole library of richly-bound French classics.

A few months later, Napoleon asked her:

" Well, were you satisfied with Fontanes ? "

" Not at all, sire, to be sure."

" How is that ? "

" He paid me in *livres ;* I would far rather have had *francs* ! "

[Pun on *livre* meaning a book, and *livre*, a coin of the value of a franc.]

Anon.   *Ces Demoiselles de l'Opéra.*

LAPORTE'S RETORT TO FANNY CERRITO

This celebrated *danseuse* was constantly exhibiting a jealousy of fancied privileges and preferences shown to Taglioni.   On her once sending back the ticket of a box (which had been given her upon an upper tier), with the remark that she was " much too young to be exalted to the skies before her proper time," M. Laporte, who had given a box on the same tier to Taglioni, replied that he " had done his best, but that possibly he had been wrong in placing the lady on the same level (*le même rang*) with Mademoiselle Taglioni."

Benjamin Lumley.   *Reminiscences of the Opera.*

THE BON-MOTS OF LEONTINE BEAUGRAND

" What can you expect ? " said someone to her the

other day, to console her. " Mlle. Sangalli dances in another language ! "

" Oh ! Oh ! " said she, " another language ! Why not say slang ! That would be more to the point."

*

One of her companions, as self-satisfied as was Vestris, the *diou de la danse*, said to her one evening in the green-room.

" Isn't it strange ! If I rise when dancing I find it quite difficult to come down again, because I'm so light ! "

" So do I," replied Beaugrand ; " I only come to the ground because the air up above tickles the soles of my feet ! "

*

A youthful companion said to her, pointing out a gentleman in evening dress

" Do you see that gentleman ? He is a minister ! And he compared me to a butterfly ! "

" Mind the pin ! " observed Beaugrand.

*

" Ah ! What a shapely foot ! Really, only Cinderella herself could have had such a small one."

" Be off with you ! " she said laughingly. " Be frank, it is the length of my nose which makes you say that ! "

*

When, in 1880, the dancer and *maître de ballet*, L. Mérante, placed Beaugrand on the retired list, on the score that she was ageing, she remarked :

" He says I am no longer young because I make him look old."

Anon. *La Vie à Paris.*

AUBRYET'S COMMENT ON LOUISE FIOCRE

On observing the gracefulness of Louise Fiocre, one of our most noted playwrights [Xavier Aubryet] cried :

" By Jove !   How I would hire that Fiocre by the hour !

[Pun on *fiacre*, a word of somewhat similar sound, meaning a cab which could be hired by the hour or journey.]

Anon.   *Ces Demoiselles de l'Opéra.*

THE LONG ARMS OF LAURE FONTA

" Do you know," said Mlle. Baratte, " why Laure never goes out when it rains, without wearing black gloves ?   Well, it is because her arms are so long that she is frightened of soiling her hands when walking."

Anon.   *Ces Demoiselles de l'Opéra.*

MLLE. LOBSTEIN

Someone asked her :
" You are German, are you not ? "
" Yes, sir."
And then she added artlessly :
" Can you see that from the stalls ? "

Anon.   *Ces Demoiselles de l'Opéra.*

ROSITA MAURI'S REVENGE

On seeing the Tsar in his box, chatting instead of watching her dancing, she grumbled :
" Well, I shall certainly not eat any more caviare ! "

Original source unknown to compiler.

ANTON DOLIN RECEIVES AN UNUSUAL COMPLIMENT

Pomona was a huge success for all concerned, and Lopokova's excitement was bubbling over.   Rushing into my dressing-room, kissing me affectionately on both cheeks, she cried : " Oh, Pat, you were beautiful, a beautiful, prancing *cantaloup* ! "

I still hope she meant antelope.

Anton Dolin.   *Divertissement.*

KSHESSINSKAYA'S RETORT TO DIAGHILEV

Kshessinskaya travelled with her own retinue and lived in the royal manner.   Diaghilev often teased her, and one evening at dinner he remarked :

" Oh Matildoshka ; yes. You are superb. You deserve all your success, even to the two Grand Dukes at your feet."

" But, Sergei Pavlovich," she answered quickly, " I have two feet."

Romola Nijinsky. *Nijinsky*.

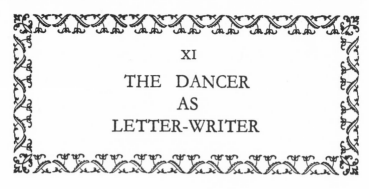

Bordeaux,
March 12th, 1785.

To——

It affords me too much pleasure to think that you like me, not to ask you to do me a kindness, and I feel sure that you will not resent the confidence I repose in you. This preamble is to inform you, Sir, that I am going to take advantage of the offer you made me, yes, undoubtedly, because no one could render greater justice to your merit, and because I shall consider myself very fortunate to animate my ballet with the fire of your pencil. I venture to beg you to loan me some costume designs for *Alexandre et Porus* and *La Caravane*, and I promise you that they will not leave my portfolio. I will restore them to you immediately on my return to Paris in the month of April, 1786, and you may be sure of my everlasting gratitude.

Did I not fear to commit an indiscretion, I would ask you to include a costume for Alzira and Ramora at the moment when the Spaniards achieve the conquest of Peru ; my wife shares in my entreaties, feeling sure that you will be pleased to help me. I shall not discuss the value I place on this service for fear of offending you, but, however little you desire, it is for you to say what sum will satisfy you and I will pay it gladly. Deign to be so kind as to favour me with a prompt reply. My ballet, *La Conquête de Pérou*, must be given after Easter so that I have not a moment to lose, those of *Alexandre et Porus* and *La Foire du Caire* will follow it immediately, and, should

I be so unfortunate as not to obtain the help I ask of you, I shall be forced to go to some fan-painter, and you can imagine how that will annoy me.

I do not know whether M. Morel ever thinks of the paltry *maître de ballet* of Bordeaux, but, if you see him, tell him that I shall be eternally grateful to him for the kindnesses he has done me, and that the man who will be his friend till death is always at his command.

Should you be so kind as to send me the designs mentioned you will greatly oblige me by addressing them to M. Dauberval, pensionnaire du Roi, at the Hotel de la Comédie, Bordeaux, and to have them taken to me at No. 63, Rue de Clery.

I shall say nothing of my successes nor of those of my wife. The citizens of Bordeaux have bestowed on us much more applause than we deserve, but we try not to follow the absurdities of the sublime Académie Royale de Musique, because there (as you know) the artistes are ferociously pestered by the fools who direct it, and I thank my lucky stars that I am far away from such a hell where counterfeit talent does not cease to be encouraged.

I am, Sir, your servant, your sincere admirer, and ever your friend,

DAUBERVAL.

Bordeaux,
August 11th, 1796.

To——

Vestris's *débuts* have taken up so much of my time that I have been unable to reply before.

You will see from the attached letter that Laborie definitely wishes to end his engagement at Bordeaux. I can praise him for keeping to his signature, and if (as I wrote to Taylor) he will not decide now to have him for the season '97 to '98 he will not have him.

I think, undoubtedly, that the mean views of the directors of the Haymarket Theatre are revolting to an artist, and that it is only in the Théâtre des Arts that I can find means to produce my works with a group of reunited talents, but the little monetary profit to be gained and the obstacles which M. Gardel erects against *maîtres de ballet* who might rival him, force me to dream of a calling that will agree with my health, for coal smoke does not suit me at all. What would you, dear and worthy citizen, an unworthy stock-holder must do what he *can* and not what he wishes.

I told Bacceli that you had sent her the papers concerning her sales.

My wife, together with your friend, send you the most grateful and respectful friendship.

DAUBERVAL.

Remember me to Mlle. Chevigny. I have made sincere vows for her re-establishment.

Paris,
the 27th ——, 1832.

To the Marquis de Maisonfort.

DEAR MARQUIS,
It is at least an age since I wrote you and gave you some particulars respecting our theatre. Doubtless you will have learned from the newspapers of the effect produced by the opera *Le Serment*,[1] and also the ballet *Nathalie*,[2] although both are too slight to set off important artistes.

The theme of *Le Serment* is absolutely nil ; I might even say that the music is equivalent, although it is composed by Aubert [*sic*] ; however, some airs in it are quite remarkable, especially a melody sung by Mme. Damoreau,[3] in which she is divine. The success of the opera is due to that piece. Apart from this, I find the opera unworthy of our theatre.

I hope Aubert [*sic*] is going to reinstate himself with a grand opera which has been commissioned two days ago. The theme is Swedish, and deals with the

[1] Opera-ballet by Halevy and C. Gide, first produced 20th June, 1832.
[2] First produced 7th November, 1832.
[3] A famous soprano.

death of Gustavus III.[1] It will be a whole evening's performance, because it is to be in five acts. This opera has already been the cause of many troubles— a lawsuit and the loss of Mme. Damoreau. She was to have played the principal part which was taken away from her after she had agreed to accept it. But at that time there was no Mlle. Falcon.[2] Since then, that young person, who is certainly very far from equalling Mme. Damoreau's inimitable talent, has made her *début* and achieved a success as Alice in *Robert*, which was sufficient to take the *rôle* from the rightful owner and give it to the newcomer. This brought tears and illness to Mme. Damoreau, who wished to break her contract. It appears, however, that all has ended for the best, for Mme. Damoreau has agreed to remain and Mlle. Falcon will sing the *rôle*. I believe the part is a dramatic one and there-fore better suited to Mlle. Falcon, although I consider it is risking a good deal to present an opera without Mme. Damoreau. I think you will agree with me.

Now I wish to speak to you about *Nathalie*. It is not an important ballet, for it has only two acts and it has been specially designed for me. In it I am neither Bayadère nor Sylphide, but a simple Swiss peasant-girl. I must admit that I did not take the part without some misgivings. It is a quite new style for me in which I am bound to find rivals, although, up to the present, I have received the most flattering commendations on my dancing.

It is only in my miming that I am conscious of some shortcomings, and that is why the part of Nathalie makes me nervous. There is a very difficult scene in the second act which I was lucky enough to bring off, and I am now said to be better than a mime, that is to say, an actress. If I were writing to anyone but you, I should not quote this praise, for I should be thought to be vain, but you know me too well to think so.

[1] *Gustave III ou le Bal Masqué,* libretto by Scribe, music by Auber; first produced 27th February, 1833.
[2] A famous soprano.

In talking of myself, I have strayed from the ballet. Some of the newspaper critics find the theme absolutely meaningless. But much praise is bestowed upon the dances and the setting, as well as the costumes, which were also devised by my father.

Fortunately for us, all the best dancers take part in the ballet. First of all, Perrot, who dances like a dream, and the Mlles. Noblet. Mme. Dupont[1] has lost a good deal since she sprained herself in *La Tentation*, and she has got stouter. Mlle. Duvernay has not been able to dance, she has a bad foot ; and nothing more is heard of all the tales that used to be told about her. I think her mother does her more harm than good. She was offered a London engagement, but her mother gave out that it would be very difficult for her to accept it, since she had offers from all the foreign Courts. I must tell you that I am not so difficult to please, for I have just signed my London contract. I shall leave early in April so as to return in July. Will you not give us the hope of seeing you soon ? No one will be more pleased than we. I trust that you have completely recovered your health. So you will not have that excuse.

Lentivi says to me every day : " When you write to the Marquis, do not forget to mention me." Mme. Rozier also wished to be remembered to you.

Good-bye, dear Marquis, with all good wishes from my father and grandmamma, and I must not forget de Voisins, or he would never forgive me. Good-bye once again and believe me ever your sincere and most affectionate friend,

MARIE.

London,
                    March 15th, 1834.

To the Marquis de la Maisonfort.

DEAR MARQUIS,

Thank you very much for your most kind letter. You are the first to tell us of the performance

---

[1] The sister of Lise Noblet. She married the singer, Pierre Auguste—called Alexis Dupont.

of *Don Juan*. I am delighted that M. Véron should have succeeded so well. Nourrit and Mlle. Falcon must be very pleased with their success, and I wager Mme. Damoreau is suffering from spleen. How Lentivi must be hating Mlle. Falcon, you know how he dislikes his favourites to owe all to others. Ernest had already told me of the *début* of M. Carrée and Mlle. Ripiquet ; I did not expect a success from the latter, and am very curious to see the former. London is not as dull as I had expected it to be at this season, but the theatre, although full, is not modish. It is not the fashion to come there until after Easter. All the most notable singers and dancers might be performing, and no one would come to hear them, and, in spite of the pleasant time I am having just now, I do not think I shall wish to return for this season next year. Also I have only danced four times, twice the Sylphide, and twice the Bayadère. My benefit is to be on the 20th with the first production of the new ballet, which I shall appear in twice only, as on the 22nd I dance for the last time. All the same, I have taken as much trouble as if I were going to dance all the time, and my father has taken great pains, too, for here, with hardly anyone, one has to do the impossible.

Mlle. Duvernay will take my part when I leave. As a dancer she has achieved a *succés d'estime* only, but as a beauty she has been an enormous success. We have Mlle. Chevigny for second dancer ; also Mlle. Kepler, who is considered extremely ugly. Little Henriot is *coryphée* ; they say that although she is small she should be a head shorter to be perfect. The great Bourgoin is looked upon as a shadow.

M. Leblond, Mme. Rozier's brother-in-law, acquits himself fairly well in any *pas* and rôle that he is given, and generally pleases. Emile, who took Mazilier's part in *La Sylphide*, is thought detestable. I am very sorry for the poor young man. Now you know everything of interest concerning our theatre. I will, however, just say a few words about Covent

Garden where they are playing *La Révolte du Sérail* and *Gustave*. I had the pleasure of seeing both. The *Révolte* is a parody of our ballet. Mlle. Leroux is very bad in it, I might even say hideous, which she certainly was not in her small part as page. She is expecting Lafont to arrive, but is, I think, consoling herself a little in his absence. Mlle. Vagon is decidedly pleasing and quite passable for her in Mlle. Duvernay's part. She is thought to be very pretty, and M. Belmont, who has just arrived, finds her most faithful and not for want of opportunity to be otherwise. However, she will hear of nothing but matrimony or ten thousand louis, and apparently neither has been offered. Mlle. Cora plays Mme. Elie's rôle. She is neither good nor bad, and has started a passionate affair here with a young lord of our acquaintance, a charming boy and deeply in love with her. Mlle. Careher is playing the page, and for the moment has several aspirants. I saw the opera *Gustave*. Nothing could be worse, and the ball at best is only worthy of Mme. Saqui ; the *Pas des Folies* is danced by Mlle. Cora. It is a most curious sight. That is all the scandal. I shall certainly not read it, as I should not send it to you, as I seem to have disparaged everyone.

Here is some important news. Mr. Bunn has engaged Mlle. Noblet, Mme. Dupont, and M. Albert for May and June. He told Alfred so himself.

This is a very long letter, and it is very late and I do not want to miss the post, so good-bye and I shall soon have the pleasure of seeing you again, as I expect to leave on Sunday the 23rd, or on the 24th at latest. We all send you our best wishes, including your most affectionate

MARIE [TAGLIONI].

P.S.—My father bids me say that he is very sorry not to have answered you, but he literally has not a moment to himself. Yesterday I bought the little summer dress you asked for. I do not know if it will please you, so you will just have to trust to my bad taste.

Paris,
                    24*th November*, 1835.

To the Marquis de Maisonfort.

My Dear Marquis,

I cannot say that lack of time has prevented my answering you ; alas, I have had only too much time on my hands. It has been the will that has been wanting, physical ills are less easily endured than mental ones. Just imagine a poor woman who is so well that she is even growing stout, who eats with a good appetite, and yet cannot move, not even from her bed to the drawing-room, because her leg is in a groove which prevents the slightest movement, and this has been going on for a month and four days. The cure makes such slow progress that I can consider myself very fortunate if I am able to walk in two months' time, after which you can guess what a task it will be to become the Sylphide again. You will realise how much I suffer ; it is a hard test of my patience. If I have any consolation, it is the interest taken in me by the public, which has always spoiled me—what will it not do when I return ! However, dear Marquis, I must say, in order to assuage your kind anxiety concerning me, that, despite the rumours being circulated that I never shall be able to dance again, a rumour doubtless inspired by some kind friends, I am assured that my leg will get well.

So I hope to give them a little disappointment. I admit that I think I am going to be a little spiteful, because it is so bad to be lazy that it makes us fall into faults.

I have nothing very much to say about our new director.[1] Poor man, I am sorry to see him there. He hasn't got the qualities necessary to manage such a place ; he shouts, loses his head, becomes insulting, makes himself ill, and all to no purpose. He is

---

[1] Duponchel, director of the *Académie Royale de Musique* from 1835-1840.

under the influence of two or three people who lead him into stupidities and yet he thinks he is cleverer than Véron ;[1] it is easy to distinguish between him who reigned for four years and him who, perhaps, will not last more than six months. I shall not speak of the manner in which he has treated me, except to say that he has not acted as a man should act towards a woman who any day can help him to earn money ; and who had the delicacy not to break off her contract the day he entered the Opéra, although he was well aware that I had the right to do so. Well, I have had my lesson, and I shall know how to make use of it and he will see that it does not do to offend people who can be useful to him. On the other hand, I must say that he is a good-natured fellow without any head and who trusts no one.

The Opéra is supported by the number of its subscribers, which has exceeded that of last year. But everyone is discontented and grumbles, and talks about Véron, who is lauded to the skies. We shall have nothing new until the end of February, when there is to be given Meyerbeer's opera, which is said to be magnificent.

Mme. Damoreau has made a superb contract with the Opéra Comique and that is all Duponchel's fault. He has made a very big mistake because Mme. Damoreau will make the Opéra Comique all the rage. He is going to give a *début* to Augusta, the protegée of M. de St. Jam[e]s. Poor little thing, she is pretty but that is absolutely all. He has also given the *Révolte*,[2] played by Pauline Leroux,[3] who was very pleasing in it, according to my father ; but there is one of my ballets sacrificed. This ballet, which up to now has brought in receipts amounting to from 6,500 to 7,000 francs, only made 4,000 the last time. The *Bayadère* is also going to be done,

---

[1] Director of the *Académie Royale de Musique* from 1831-1835.
[2] *La Révolte au Sérail*, ballet by P. Taglioni, music by T. Labarre.
[3] A celebrated dancer of the period. She became *première danseuse de demi-caractère* in 1841.

with my neighbour Mlle. Noblet in the title-rôle.
There is only the *Sylphide* left now to be sacrificed.
Even now, I can see that it will end in Véron's being
implored on hands and knees to take over the Opéra
again. However, he has said that he will never re-
assume management ; but a golden bridge will be
made and men are weak. There, dear Marquis, I
have told you all my news. Mme. Razin, whom I
saw yesterday, told me that she will write you a diary
of all that is going on, so I hope to arrive before her,
because I haven't the strength to struggle. I always
see too little of her, she has so many new acquaint-
ances that the old ones must be a little neglected on
their account.

Lentivi has much trouble in dragging himself
along ; he suffers a great deal from his legs, and sees
so few people. He wearies of everything now his
Elsslers aren't here. As for Meynadier, I believe
he is going to be successful in a new enterprise
which he is about to begin and for which he has already disposed of sixty shares. My brother and
sister-in-law are well. They received some very
beautiful presents from the Emperor of Russia during
their visit to Kalisch ; what, for instance, is not so
fortunate for them is that there will soon be a further
increase in their family. It seems to me that they
should have been satisfied with two.

If you only knew how pleasantly surprised I was
yesterday to see your sister, who was so kind and
pleasant to me and put herself out on purpose ! And
how happy I was to receive a visit from your mother !
She seems very well. We hope then to see you in
January. It is a long while ahead but it is something
to look forward to. I hope then soon to meet you.

My father and mother wish me to send you their
affectionate regards. With all this chatter I have
forgotten to mention your health. So you have been
ill, your sister told me. Come and see us and the
Paris air will completely restore you. Do forgive
me for not knowing when to stop. When once I

K

begin—but there, you know what gossips women are.

Good-bye,

With kindest regards,

MARIE TAGLIONI.

Paris,

Friday, the 12th——

To the Marquis de Maisonfort.

DEAR MARQUIS,

I keep my word as you see. I could not write to you yesterday. I was too tired and obliged to receive visitors. What a pity you could not be here on Wednesday ! I am sure that you, our good friend, would have been very pleased to see that gala, because I cannot describe that performance other than as a gala.

Imagine a theatre packed to capacity, full of lovely dresses, and 10,121 francs in M. Duponchel's treasury. Three rows of the pit had to be turned into stalls. As you know, when the curtain rises, I am kneeling, and no sooner was I seen than the applause became so overwhelming that I was obliged to rise and bow my acknowledgements. After my *pas* in the second act, I was recalled and bouquets were thrown from all the boxes. Half of them fell into the stalls where they were picked up and thrown on to the stage. It really was very pretty and at the end of the ballet I was again recalled. I doubt if there has ever been a performance quite the same, it was the nicest one I have known up to now. The King of Naples and all the Royal Family were present.

You must forgive me, dear Marquis, for writing in so immodest a strain, but you know that I am not vainer, only very happy, because that day I risked all my reputation ; so, dear Marquis, I have written you the truth and nothing but the truth.

To complete my happiness, on Wednesday, at nine in the morning, my brother and sister-in-law arrived, but they only stop for a week. Dear

Marquis, doubtless you will have received my letter of the day before yesterday. My father and mother desire me to give you their best wishes.

Remember me to the one who is dear to you.

Always yours sincerely,
M. TAGLIONI.

Berlin,
February 17th, 1834.

To M. Lormier.

MY DEAR LORMIER,

Enclosed I send you the exact model of the costume worn by my daughter in my ballet *Satanella*, the costume which M. St. Léon, in a letter full of rancour against me, published in *La Revue et Gazette des Théâtres*, declares to have been copied from that of his little imp in *Le Violon du Diable*. You must admit that this is an outrageous assumption of that gentleman's, and entirely unfounded. But, as I have proved the falsity of his allegations, I shall be much obliged if, in order to complete my defence, you would be so kind as to send a line to M. Pommereux, editor of the said periodical, stating that you are in a position to certify that the costume of the little imp in *Le Violon du Diable* and that of Satanella in the ballet of the same name have no resemblance whatsoever. I shall be most grateful if you would do this immediately.

Yours sincerely,
PAUL TAGLIONI.

Sunday.

To——

SIR,

Although the praise of a woman who is unversed in letters must afford little gratification to so distinguished a writer, I cannot believe, Sir, that my admiration for your charming book is displeasing to you.

When I—an artist—am applauded, I do not try to

discover from which corner of the house the applause comes, and whose hands are responsible.

With my best wishes,

Very truly yours,

AMALIA FERRARIS.

71, *Haymarket*,
[*London*]
Thursday, July 1st.

To——

MY DEAR FIORENTINO,

I have just received your charming, but all too brief, letter. If I waited until to-day to write to you, it was because I had no good news to send. Always *Esmeralda* or *Giselle*. But, since Saturday last, we have at last given the *Pas des Quatre Elements*. I think this is one of Perrot's best compositions. Cerrito represented Air ; Rosati, Water ; and I, Fire. We have each a separate entry, then a scene in which Water rushes to extinguish Fire ; this is short but very pretty. Afterwards comes the *pas* in which I make my entrance out of a flame, which is most effective, as it all takes place so quickly that no one can understand how I arrive on the stage. Then I have a very brilliant *variation* which procures me an immediate and magnificent success. As to the actual *pas*, if I am not mistaken and from what I hear, it is I who have made the greatest success of the three. I dance a good deal with Cerrito, which she does not like very much, although it pleases me. We have a *variation* together in the *allégro* part of the *pas*, which we always have to repeat. This *pas* has been very helpful to the success of the performance, because, even without Lind, we have had two magnificent houses, and the Queen has honoured us with her presence. Taglioni is expected hourly, and, as soon as she arrives, we shall revive the *Pas de Quatre* of two years past.

If the Paris Opéra closes, I think I shall stay a few more days in London, perhaps even a month. This

I am anxious to do, as dancing is turning out so well that by remaining a little longer I hope to increase my reputation. It is the talk here that Pillet has left and that Rocplan[1] [*sic*] has the theatre, but I cannot believe it now. It has been talked about for so long that I have given up all hope.

Good-bye, my dear Fiorentino, I trust in you as I hope you trust in me, to be always your very devoted friend.

CARLOTTA GRISI.

[1] Nestor Roqueplan was co-director, with Duponchel, of the Académie Royale de Musique from 1847–48, when the latter retired and Roqueplan became sole director, retaining the post until 1854.

XII

DANCERS' NICKNAMES

LA REINE DE LA DANSE
(The Queen of Dancing)

Nickname given to Mlle. La Fontaine, the first *danseuse* to appear on the stage of the Paris Opéra.

LA PRINCESSE
(The Princess)

Nickname given to Mlle. Mariette, in tribute to the influence wielded by her as the mistress of the Prince de Carignan, who was appointed Inspector-General of the Opéra in 1731.

LE GRAND DUPRÉ
(The Tall Dupré)

Nickname given to Louis Dupré, who was tall, to distinguish him from an inferior dancer of the same name—Jean Denis Dupré.

LE DIEU DE LA DANSE
(The God of Dancing)

This nickname was borne in turn by three celebrated dancers : Louis Dupré, Gaetano Vestris, and Auguste Vestris. Dupré received this nickname in tribute to the dignity and precision of his dancing. When he retired from the stage, his famous pupil, Gaetano Vestris, acquired the title. It is said that one night, when he was dancing at the Opéra, and acclaimed by his brothers and sisters, who took every opportunity to be present on such occasions in order to swell the applause with their own contributions, one of his brothers, Gian Battista, who spoke French with a marked Italian accent, cried out in a moment of enthusiasm : " *C'est le Diou de la Danse !* " The phrase passed through the audience and henceforth Gaetano Vestris became the " *diou* " *de la danse*. In turn, as his son, Auguste, proved his greatness as a dancer, he transferred his title to him.

MALTER LE DIABLE, MALTER L'OISEAU, MALTER L'ANGLAIS

(Malter the Devil, Malter the Bird, Malter the Englishman)

In 1734 there were three dancers of secondary rôles at the Opéra, who bore the name of Malter. They were brothers and distinguished from one another by particular nicknames. The eldest, C. Malter, was known as Malter *le Diable*, because he danced demon parts. The next in age, L. Malter, was called Malter *l'Oiseau*, in tribute to the lightness of his dancing. The youngest of all was styled Malter *l'Anglais*, possibly because he went to London to dance with Marie Sallé during her season at the Lincoln's Inn Fields Theatre, 1733–4. He is also known as Malter III and Malter *la Petite Culotte* (Malter with the breeches), but the writer has been unable to trace the origin of this nickname.

L'APOLLON DE LA DANSE
(The Apollo of Dancing)

Nickname given to Charles Le Picq, in tribute to his noble features, excellent physique, and fine technique.

LA VÉNUS DE MEDICI DE LA DANSE
(The Venus de Medici of Dancing)

Nickname given to Mlle. Miller, afterwards the wife of Pierre Gardel, in tribute to the beautiful proportions of her body.

LA SQUELETTE DES GRÂCES
(The Skeleton of the Graces)

Nickname given to Madeleine Guimard on account of her extreme thinness.

LA DÉSOSSÉE
(The Boneless)

Nickname given to Mlle. Gosselin in tribute to her extreme flexibility.

PAUL L'AÉRIEN
(Paul the Aerial)

Nickname given to Paul in tribute to his wonderful elevation. Ebers (*Seven Years of the King's Theatre*) declares that " he actually seemed to fly as he bounded from the stage, so light and zephyry were his motions."

PERROT L'AÉRIEN
(Perrot the Aerial)

Paul's nickname was transferred to Jules Perrot, in tribute to his unusual elevation.

LA DÉESSE DE LA DANSE
(The Goddess of Dancing)

Nickname given to Marie Taglioni in tribute to the beauty of her dancing.

XIII

SOME FASHIONS AND TRADE-MARKS INSPIRED BY DANCERS

MARIE CAMARGO

On May 5th, 1726, Camargo made her *début* at the Paris Opéra with great success in *Les Caractères de la Danse*, a series of *divertissements* originally composed by Rebel for Mlle. Prévost. The newcomer added to her laurels a few weeks later when she appeared, first, as a Matelotte in Menesson's *Ajax*, and then as a Grace in Fuzelier's ballet, *Les Amours Déguisés* ; and, as a result, she became the rage. Hairdressers invented *coiffures à la Camargo*, milliners brought out dresses, mantillas and sleeves *à la Camargo*, and her shoemaker, Choisy, reaped a golden harvest with his shoes *à la Camargo*, for the dancer's foot, being unusually small, it was thought that this enviable quality might be acquired by wearing similar shoes.

MADELEINE GUIMARD

In 1771 the *robe à la Guimard* made its appearance. This was the name given to a frock of one colour, caught up to reveal a petticoat of a different shade, trimmed with pompons and garlands, like the costume worn by Guimard as Creüse, in Noverre's *Jason et Medée*.

SALVATORE VIGANÒ

When Salvatore Viganò and his wife, Maria Medina, danced at Vienna towards 1793, they achieved a furore, which gave rise to shoes and *coiffures à la Viganò*.

Even Beethoven wrote a Menuet *à la Viganò*,

which was danced by the Signora Venturini and Signor Checchi in Heubel's *Le Nozze Disturbante*, presented at the Schikander Theatre, Vienna, on May 18th, 1795.

MARIE TAGLIONI

This celebrated dancer's success in *La Sylphide*, in which she wore the dress of white muslin designed by Eugène Lami, which became the traditional costume of the classical ballet, led to a demand for dresses made of that material, and fashionable ladies adorned their costumes with a profusion of ribbons to make them ethereal with their flutterings and rustlings.

During the Paris season of 1834–35 the famous Maison Maurice Beauvais brought out a *Turban Sylphide* in honour of Taglioni.

In England the dancer's success was marked by the association of her name and principal rôle with articles of a utilitarian nature. The periodicals of the 'forties often contain advertisements inserted by Messrs. E. Moses & Son, of 154, Minories, offering ready-made Taglionis (a short overcoat), in tweed from 8*s*. 6*d*., or with velvet collar and cuffs, lined throughout, from 9*s*. Another firm, Messrs. W. & J. Sangster, of 140, Regent Street, draw attention to their " La Sylphide " parasol, the merit of which is that it " can be closed instantaneously, without moving either hand."

As an instance of how fashions often spring from the most delicate of impulses, it is of interest to quote the following story recounted by Miss Mabel Cross, in her account of Marie Taglioni (*University Magazine*, April, 1879). " In Paris, she [Taglioni] was going one night to the opera, and took out fresh from its box a new hat just received from her *modiste*, Mme. Alexandre Baudrant, a celebrity of the day. This was in the time when ladies wore hats at the opera ; and her new hat, being very pretty, of a fine and delicate straw, she straightway put it on for the occasion. A few days afterwards her milliner came to her in consternation. ' Madame Taglioni, what have you been doing ? I turned back the brim of your hat, because it was so delicate, that it might not be hurt in the box, and you have worn it so at the opera ! ' ' Oh ! ' said Taglioni, ' I supposed it was a new fashion.' And so it was, Taglioni having worn it ; next week all the ladies went to the opera with hats turned back at the brim."

FANNY ELSSLER

Following upon Fanny Elssler's triumphant *début* at Paris on September 15th, 1834, in *La Tempête* (a ballet arranged by Coralli to a theme based on the play by Shakespeare), the famous shop in the Rue Sainte-Anne, Les Grands Magasins du Temple du Goût, brought out *elsslerine*, " a transparent material, carrying a thin lining, for ballroom and evening dresses, and manufactured by a new process."

Elssler's successful tour of America in 1840–42 procured her inclusion in the series of " portrait " bottles—glass whisky-flasks with one side containing a representation in bas relief of a notable person of the period—which were very popular in the 'forties in America. Elssler is represented full-length, dancing.

ANNA PAVLOVA

The immense popularity of this dancer gave rise to Pavlova cigarettes, Pavlova perfume, Pavlova powder, and Pavlova stockings.

VASLAV NIJINSKY

At the first performance by the Diaghilev Company at Paris (17th May, 1909) Nijinsky appeared as the Slave in *Le Pavillon d'Armide*. The 18th century costume designed for him by A. Benois included a jewelled collar originally intended to rest on the top edge of his coat. Nijinsky, however, raised the necklace so that it formed a band round his neck. This innovation was remarked and admired, and led to a new fashion in necklaces—*à l'Armide*—chokers of black *moiré* set off with diamonds and pearls.

FIRST APPEARANCE OF FANNY ELSSLER IN AMERICA
(Park Theatre, New York, May 14th, 1840)

Many and many a night has passed since the walls of the Park have witnessed such a scene. Fanny Elssler, the bright star whose rising in our firmament has been anxiously looked for by the fashionable astronomers since its transit across the ocean was announced, shone forth in all its brilliancy this evening. Her reception was the warmest and most enthusiastic I ever witnessed. On her first appearance, in a *pas seul* called *La Cracovienne*, which was admirably adapted to set off her fine figure to advantage, the pit rose in a mass, and the waves of the great animated ocean were capped by hundreds of white pocket handkerchiefs. . . .

Then came the ballet, *La Tarentule*, in which the Elssler established her claim to be considered by far the best dancer we have ever seen in this country. At the falling of the curtain she was called out ; the pit rose in a body and cheered her, and a shower of wreaths and bouquets from the boxes proclaimed her success complete. She appeared greatly overcome by her reception, and coming to the front of the stage, pronounced, in a tremulous voice, in broken English, the words " a thousand thanks," the *naïveté* of which seemed to rivet the hold she had gained on the affections of the audience. . . . The house, although full in every part, was not crowded, and a more respectable audience never greeted the fair *danseuse* in any country she has charmed.

Philip Hone. *Diary.*

THE GREEN-ROOM AT THE OPÉRA, PARIS, IN THE EIGHTEEN-FORTIES

This green-room, which still bears the rich remains of former painting and gilding, was once the saloon of the Duke de Choiseul ; it has seen more serious magnificence before becoming the asylum of these choregraphical splendours. On entering, your first care must be to uncover yourself, and to keep your hat in your hand, for by an ingenious fiction, once in the green-room, you are in the house of the King, not the constitutional King of the French, but better still, in that cf His Majesty Louis XV., a King who, of all his dynasty, has preserved nothing but the etiquette with which he pensioned the green-room ; thus any ill-bred Frenchman has a right, not to salute His Majesty Louis Philippe as he passes, and to refuse the Queen a bow, but no one may keep on his hat before these Opéra ladies, who, however, will take care not to acknowledge your civility. They will scarcely bestow a side glance upon the stranger who presents himself in the comic kingdom ; you, however, who are wise, when you see these ladies so occupied with their *jetés battus*, will forget your intended conquests, and indeed you are quite right, for all of them—the ugliest and the most beautiful, she for whom the public waits to throw at her feet its delight and its homage, and she whose name it will never know—are fully engaged, without asking you who you are. At this moment, they belong to the public, he is their only master, they think of no one but him, they would give all their love, past, present, and to come, for a round of applause, or even less than that, for a favourable murmur ; so that if, in the green-room, you fancy yourself in the presence of simple anacreontic divinities, you are in great error ; you are in the presence of women who sing or who dance. However, your choice is soon made, you return to what you were a short time since, an attentive spectator, but a spectator in the first boxes ; and now your amusement is to recognise them one after another : the elegant Fanny Elssler, in her Spanish costume, half silk, half lace, without speaking of the brown skin which is seen through this light dress ; Pauline Leroux calm and pensive ; Carlotta Grisi light and active ; the two Noblets ; the beautiful Dumilâtre ; with the subalterns, who are not the least pretty ; and around these stars, the wandering satellites ; —this one obtains a smile, that one a look, another is acknowledged almost as a conqueror—but silence ! The dance is called for, the public waits and is impatient ; at this signal, these birds with brilliant plumage fly off, uttering a little cry of joy ; they fly light as air, and in this saloon, recently so full, nothing remains, unless it is a flower fallen from the figure, a ringlet unfastened from the long hair, a pinion which has broken off, all sorts of appointments, jokes, love-pledges, and nothings ; but they, the sylphides, what are they now doing ?   They accompany the sylphs into the air, they repose in the old palace of the Sleeping Beauty in the wood, they swim into the azure grottoes of the Daughter of the Danube ;   they have introduced revolt into the seraglio of the Grand Seignior, disordered revelling into the ruined monastery of Robert le Diable ; wherever they go, they carry with a bird's flight every passion and every love.

Jules Janin.   *The American in Paris.*

DRESSING-ROOM OF THE CORPS DE BALLET
(*Circa* 1845)

The ballet girl has entered the house by the stage-door ; and, with a nod to the hall-keeper to show him that she is there if a bouquet has been sent, and a glance at the rack for a letter, she goes to her room.

Five other sylphs attire with her ; and the room has two long dressers against its sides, divided into compartments, each containing a common looking-glass and a few mysterious pomatum and rouge-pots, combs, powder-dabbers, scraps of silver leaves, and

" logics," and a wash-hand stand in the middle. And then the toilet commences, and the dancer has a hard time of it. For the waist of the dress is too short, or the skirts too long, or the white comes below the tarlatan, or the wings won't fit well at all to the shoulders, but droop down as if they were going to fall off like those of the Mountain Sylph. And such phrases as : " Fasten the top hook and eye, Kate " ; or, " Pin my scarf, Loo, there's a dear "; or, " Am I all right behind ?   Do tell me, Laura ! with similar ones, are rapidly and unceasingly uttered, until the call-boy walks down the corridor, shouting : " Overture's begun, ladies ! "

Albert Smith. *Natural History of the Ballet Girl.*

THE CORPS DE BALLET AT REHEARSAL
(*Circa* 1845)

" Now, ladies ! ladies ! " cried the ballet-master knocking a tambourine, " we are behind time. Places ! places ! "

And the army gets into order, each taking her gun or other weapon, from a bundle leaning against the side of the proscenium, and shouldering it, in her bonnet and shawl.

" Miss Saunders, where's your gun ? " asked the ballet-master, whose eagle eye detects an unarmed Amazon.

" Please, sir, it's not finished yet," is the reply.

" Very well ; take this wand."

And the ballet-master gives her a magician's rod with a serpent twisted round it—a canvas ell stuffed with sawdust and painted—and a Chinese march begins.

The ballet-master is now all excitement. Every time he bangs the tambourine, it is a signal for them to turn, or divide, simultaneously ; and they wait for the same signal at night. At last Miss Saunders gets out of step.

" Stop ! *stop ! !* STOP ! ! ! " roars the master.

But orchestral accompaniments and ballet girls are as bad to pull up, when once off, as cats without check-strings. At last, by stamping and thumping the ground with his stick, he succeeds.

" Now, if you please : once more, Mr. Barnard " [the violinist].

And Mr. Barnard begins again.

" Now, then ! " shouts the master, " what are you gaping there for ? Why don't you move ? *Why— the—devil—don't—you—move !* "   [More thumps on the stage.]   " Once more, Mr. Barnard."

At length Miss Saunders, in extreme terror, by dint of careful counting, begins to know something about it.

Albert Smith. *Natural History of the Ballet Girl.*

LOPOKOVA AND THE FIRST PERFORMANCE OF " LA BOUTIQUE FANTASQUE "

(Alhambra Theatre, London, June 5th, 1919)

On the first performance every seat had been taken and the promenades filled to overflowing. Everywhere one looked, there was the same shimmer of white faces, now and again rendered hazy by the smoke from nervously-lighted cigarettes which rose upward like incense burnt in honour of some goddess of ancient mythology. It was the symbol of the triumph that awaited Lopokova.

Behind the scenes there was a sense of nervous calm.   Derain was passing in review the dancers as they emerged from their dressing-rooms. He was very particular on the subject of *make-up* and each artist had placed on his or her table a tiny sketch showing what was required.   There was a shout of *orchestre !* and to the shrill scraping of bows, Defosse threaded his way through the musicians and took his seat.   Three metallic raps of his baton on the iron frame of his desk and there commenced the lively, pizzicato notes of the Marche Slav which forms the overture. The heavy curtain swung aloft to reveal the drop-curtain. The naïve treatment of the two figures posed against the broad masses of harmonious reds and browns recalled the decoration of an early Victorian pencil-box. One received an impression of complete, all-satisfying joy. One felt conscious of that youthful, delicious happiness experienced when on a seaside holiday one takes off one's shoes and stockings, and paddles in the sea.

The drop-curtain rose and there was the shop—bathed in the warm sunlight that streamed through the windows. The customers arrived and the dolls were brought out and set in motion. The applause was unceasing. It came in volleys of hand-claps, of stamps of the feet, which died away only to be renewed with greater vigour. When the Can-can dancers appeared there were shouts of " Lopokova ! " " Massine ! "

Lopokova was delightful. She was attired in a blue satin bodice and short, white satin skirt, fringed with black lace and stuffed with innumerable frilly petticoats ; her hair was dressed in the little curls fashionable during the Second Empire and bound with a garland of cornflowers and marguerites. Her resemblance to a doll was extraordinary. It was a totally different conception from the angular, stiffly-jointed puppet of the Ballerina in *Petrouchka*. Her rounded limbs, pale face, full cheeks, curved pouting lips and innocent expression recalled one of those china dolls at once the supreme joy of children and dread of care-worn fathers.

Not only was the resemblance complete ; her very action, her very pose was subordinated to the demands of the character. She danced with in-credible precision and verve. One leg flew upwards to writhe, twist, turn and revolve amid a sea of foaming lace and ribbon. She flaunted her petticoats in the most mischievous abandon and, without altering the expression of her features, contrived to convey by the pose of her head and arms, the fleeting

L

emotions of disdain, surrender, coquetry and pique. I have never heard a theatre resound to greater applause.

I need not recall the many other moments of rapture provided by the art of Lopokova which are revived with each performance of this ballet. It was a complete success. But Derain was frightened at the warmth of his welcome and had to be dragged upon the stage. Massine made repeated graceful bows while Lopokova, half-laughing, half-crying, seemed divided between sadness and delight.

C. W. Beaumont. *Fanfare*, December, 1921.

A REHEARSAL OF " THE SLEEPING PRINCESS "

(Winter, 1921)

You enter the Alhambra Theatre on a rehearsal night, about 8 p.m. The auditorium is without lights, empty, cold, gloomy—altogether cheerless. Seated in the stalls are at the most a dozen people. You will recognise the broad back of Diaghilev ; to his right, Léon Bakst, dapper, keen, leaning forward with his chin supported on the back of the fauteuil in front of him ; to his left, Stravinsky, coat-collar turned up and felt hat pulled over his eyes. Next to him is the *chorégraphe* Sergeyev, short, spare, and grim of expression.

Only the stage is lit, and here are grouped the members of the company. Everyone looks very cold. The costumes are varied to an infinite degree. The ladies wear pink *maillot* and short ballet-skirts, generally white ; the men tight-fitting black knickers, white shirts, white socks, and black shoes. The former have many ingenious devices for protection against the cold winds that sweep about the theatre— woollen stockings with the feet cut off make excellent gaiters, while wrapped about their shoulders are woollen cardigans and jumpers ; some wear as many as three. Others have borrowed the men's short coats. To the right of the stage, where later will

be the " wings " is a piano. Near by is the stage-
manager Grigoriev, very tall and suave, who seems
unable to move without a graceful inclination of his
body or an expressive sweep of his arms. A little
distance from him stands Nijinska in a long, black
cloak. She has a pale face and big, slanting eyes
framed in straw-coloured hair. To glance at her is
to be reminded of her famous brother. Their
movements and actions are extraordinarily similar.

The pianist renders the theme of the movement,
which echoes strangely in the vast empty space, while
the dancers perform evolution after evolution which
Nijinska controls and directs with dramatic gestures
of her arms. The dancers swirl into long, sinuous
lines, melt into one throbbing mass, divide, form
circles, revolve and then dash from sight.

Meanwhile Diaghilev consults with his lieutenants.
Sergeyev whispers that such a group might be im-
proved thus. Stravinsky is displeased with the *tempo* ;
it must be accelerated, and he emphasises his remarks
with a flourish of his cigarette. Bakst regards everything with a cold, penetrating glance. He says
little, and when he does speak, pronounces each
word with a precise intonation and very definite
significance. He has the air of a prosecuting counsel.

Now and again Diaghilev rises from his seat,
throws off his long overcoat, pulls it over his shoulders
and strides towards the footlights. He regards the
scene with his head curiously inclined to one side,
then he sharply claps his hands. The dancers cease.
He shields his mouth with his hands and shouts
directions to the stage-manager, who transfers his
instructions to the troupe. It is extraordinary how
difficult it is to make the voice carry from the auditorium to the stage. The dance is repeated with the
prescribed alterations. Presently the dancers, panting from their exertions, are permitted to rest. In
little whispering groups they walk to the " wings."
Now it is a *pas seul*. Lopokova steps forward,
dressed in a white ballet-skirt, brown stockings pulled

over her *maillot*, and her fair hair bound with a broad ribbon. She dances with a precise technique and such piquant vivacity as to draw from the famous critics a loud " bravo ! " a high mark of appreciation. She smiles, crosses one hand over her breast, and makes a mock obeisance. The *corps de ballet* resume their labours.

C. W. Beaumont. *Rehearsing The Alhambra Ballet.*
(*Dancing Times*, December, 1921.)

BEHIND THE SCENES AT THE BALLET
AS A SUBJECT FOR THE PAINTER

A ballet observed from the " wings," from the box of the limelight operator, from the " flies," or from the angle made by the backcloth and its adjacent " wing," is a totally different spectacle from that witnessed by the audience. I would say that it is far more wonderful and far more beautiful. I would say that even Nature, in all its varied expression, cannot surpass the variety and beauty of the images presented to the person privileged to stand " behind the scenes." I do not think it is an exaggeration to state that if it were possible to reproduce the subjects for pictures that occur to the mind during one single evening's performance, an artist could spend a lifetime in transferring those impressions to paper or canvas. Those unfortunate mortals who have never been on the stage—during, for example, a performance of a ballet of the Diaghilev company—can form no conception of the wonderful compositions that lie ready to hand—the entrancing beauty of co-mingled beams of coloured light, with their myriad reflections on the dresses and limbs of the dancers ; the tense attitude of the dancer awaiting her entry ; the spectral figures of the attendant dressers encumbered with shawls, cloaks, powder-puffs and glasses of water ; the terrific leap through the " wings " as a dancer makes her exit ; the grotesque appearance of a closely-viewed painted face ; the little groups of men and women exercising, conversing, or moistening parched lips with a sliced orange ; the bird-like resemblance of a short-skirted dancer who, with both feet on the ground, bends her body to tie her shoe ; the marvellous ever-changing shadows . . . Then the scenes in the dressing-rooms ; the stairs crowded with eager or tired, panting girls as they stream to and from the stage ; the setting of the scenes with the scurry of stage-hands ; the great stretches of canvas which leap upwards while others tumble down ; the ropes which hurtle through the air like maddened snakes. . . . What magnificent material !

C. W. Beaumont. *Some New Paintings of the Russian Ballet* (*Dancing World*, June, 1922).

XV

BOUQUETS

MARIE CAMARGO

De Camargo, de Salé, de Roland
Maint connaisseur exalte le talent.
Salé, dit l'un, l'emporte par la grâce ;
Roland, dit l'autre, excelle en enjouement.
Et chacun voit avec étonnement
Les pas hardis, la noble et vive audace
      De Camargo.
Entre les trois, la victoire balance,
Mais si j'étais le berger fabuleux,
Je ne sçais quoy de grand, de merveilleux,
Me forcerait à couronner la danse
      De Camargo.
      Hardouin. *Mercure de France*,
              September, 1732.

MARIE CAMARGO

Fidèle aux lois de la cadence.
Je forme au gré de l'art les pas les plus hardis ;
Originale dans ma danse,
Je puis le disputer aux Balons, aux Blondis.
      De la Faye. *Verses beneath an engraving*
            of Mlle. Camargo.

MARIE CAMARGO AND MARIE SALLÉ

Ah ! Camargo, que vous êtes brillante !
Mais que Sallé, grands dieux, est ravissante !
Que vos pas sont légers et que les siens sont doux !
Elle est inimitable et vous êtes nouvelle :
Les Nymphes sautent comme vous,
Mais les Grâces dansent comme elle.
      Voltaire. *Mercure de France*, January, 1732.

LOUIS DUPRÉ

Lorsque le grand Dupré, d'une marche hautaine,
Orné de son panache, avançoit sur la scène,
On croyoit voir un dieu demander des autels,
Et venir se mêler aux danses des mortels.
Dans tous ses déploîments sa danse simple et pure
N'étoit qu'un doux accord des dons de la nature.

C. J. Dorat. La Déclamation.

TERESA VESTRIS

Se montrer et bientôt séduire,
Aux attraits joindre les talens,
Remplir le cœur d'un aimable délire,
Charmer les yeux et captiver les sens :
Des grâces, du plaisir être la vive image :
Vestris, partager leur encens,
Que pourriez-vous désirer davantage ?
Mais je ne sais qu'ébaucher le portrait
De ces charmes qu'en vous on admire sans cesse :
Ah ! j'en suis trop rempli pour que dans son ivresse
Mon esprit enchanté les rende trait pour trait.
Comment donc aujourd'hui, nouvelle Terpsichore,
Essayer de vous peindre encore ?
Comment oser vous célébrer
Telle que je vous vois, lorsqu'au public avide
De vous voir, de vous admirer,
Vous accourez d'un vol rapide,
Le contraindre à vous adorer ?
Que de grâce ! que de noblesse !
Quelle aimable variété !
Tantôt c'est Daphné dont l'adresse
Evite un amant redouté ;
Tantôt c'est la tendre jeunesse
Dans les bras de la volupté.
L'Amour vif et léger que retient la mollesse,
Semble guider vos moindres mouvemens ;
Tel Zéphir amoureux aux beaux jours du printemps,
Agite tendrement la rose qu'il caresse.
Quels plaisirs je goûtois, Dieux ! à me retracer

Les divers sentimens qu'en moi vous faites noître,
   Quand tout à coup je vous vis paroître,
   Et près de moi l'autre jour vous placer !
De mon âme déjà par votre danse émue,
Je sentis à l'instant redoubler les transports :
  Je voulais yous parler, mais ma voix retenue
    Tenta d'inutiles efforts.
    Cependant, ô bonheur extrême !
Damis pour vous me ravit un bouquet :
   Je n'osais vous l'offrir moi-même :
Et de moi seul, blâmant son stratagème,
   Vous le reçûtes en effet.
   Enhardi par cet avantage,
J'allois vous présenter un don d'un plus haut prix ;
   Mais vos yeux me l'avoient surpris,
Quand je voulus vous en offrir l'hommage.
    Anon. *Mercure de France*, July, 1756.

MARIE ALLARD

Que n'ai-je le génie et le pinceau d'Apelle !
Allard ! à mes esprits ce tableau te rappelle.
Jamais nymphe des bois n'eut tant d'agilité ;
Toujours l'essaim des ris voltige à ton côté.
Que tu mélanges bien, ô belle enchanteresse,
La force avec la grâce, et l'aisance et l'adresse !
Tu sais avec tant d'art entremêler tes pas
Que l'œil ne peut les suivre et ne les confond pas.
Le papillon s'envole avec moins de vitesse,
Et pèse plus que toi sur les fleurs qu'il caresse.
       C. J. Dorat. *La Déclamation.*

ANNE HEINEL

Dans tous ses mouvemens quelle âme douce et fière !
Parmi le chœur dansant autour d'elle empressé,
Elle paroît, s'élève et tout est éclipsé.
La mortelle n'est plus, j'encense la déesse,
Hébé pour la fraîcheur, Pallas pour la noblesse.
Elle imprime à ses pas je ne sais quoi d'altier
Et l'oeil qui l'admira ne la peut oublier.
       C. J. Dorat. *La Déclamation.*

LOUISE LANY

Aux talens naturels que l'art soit réuni ;
Telle est à nos regards la danse de Lani.
Précision, vitesse, esprit, tout s'y rassemble,
Les détails sont parfaits, sans altérer l'ensemble.
Elle enchante l'oreille et ne l'égare pas.
La valeur de la note est toujours dans ses pas.

C. J. Dorat. *La Déclamation.*

JEAN GEORGES NOVERRE

Du feu de son génie il anima la Danse :
Aux beaux jours de la Grèce il sut la rappeler ;
Et recouvrant par lui leur antique éloquence ;
Les gestes et les pas aprirent à parler.

B. Imbert. *Verses beneath an engraving
of Noverre by Roger after Guérin.*

MARIE ALLARD AND DAUBERVAL
(*Pas de deux* in *Silvie*, 1766)

Te peindre c'est louer ton émule divin ;
Je place au même rang la Nymphe et le Silvain ;
Il partage l'honneur de ta palme brillante ;
Hippomène à la course égaloit Atalante.
Tous deux dans cette arène où vous régnez sur moi,
Vous cueillez le laurier ; mais la palme est pour
toi.

C. J. Dorat. *La Déclamation.*

MLLE. THÉODORE (MME. DAUBERVAL)

Que tu possèdes bien l'art d'attirer les cœurs !
Notre âme est dans nos yeux quand ils suivent tes
traces ;
Horace te voyoit lorsqu'il peignoit les Grâces
Dénouant leur ceinture et dansant sur les fleurs.
Charmante Dauberval, orne longtemps la scène !
Enchante un peuple gai dont tu fais les beaux jours.
J'accuse le destin qui loin de toi m'entraîne ;
Il faut ne pas te voir, ou bien te voir toujours.

Léonard.

MADELEINE GUIMARD

(As Mélite in *Le Premier Navigateur*)

Quelle nymphe légère, à mes yeux se présente !
Déesse, elle folâtre et n'est point imposante,
Son front s'épanouit avec sérénité.
Ses cheveux sont flottants, le rire est sa beauté.
D'un feston de jasmin, sa tête est couronnée,
Et sa robe voltige, aux vents abandonnée.
Mille songes légers l'environnent toujours ;
Plus que le printemps même, elle fait les beaux
   jours.
Des matelots joyeux, rassemblés auprès d'elle
Détonnent à sa gloire une ronde nouvelle,
Et de jeunes pasteurs, désertant les hameaux,
Viennent la saluer aux sons des chalumeaux.
C'est l'aimable gaîté : qui peut la méconnaître,
Au chagrin qui s'envole, aux jeux qu'elle fait naître ?
Fille de l'innocence, image du bonheur,
Le charme qui te suit, a passé dans mon cœur.
Sur ce gazon fleuri qu'elle a choisi pour trône,
Pasteurs, exécutons les danses qu'elle ordonne.

*

Fuyez, arrêtez-vous, suspendez votre ivresse ;
Comme Guimard enfin appelez les désirs,
Et que vos pas brillants soient le vol des plaisirs.

             C. J. Dorat. *La Déclamation.*

AVDOTIA ISTOMINA

The house is crammed.   A thousand lamps
On pit, stalls, boxes, brightly blaze,
Impatiently the gallery stamps,
The curtain now they slowly raise.
Obedient to the magic strings,
Brilliant, ethereal, there springs
Forth from the crowd of nymphs surrounding
Istomina the nimbly-bounding.
With one foot resting on its tip
Slow circling round its fellow swings

And now she skips and now she springs
Like down from Ælous's lip,
Now her lithe form she arches o'er
And beats with rapid foot the floor.

*

Shouts of applause !

> Pushkin. *Eugene Onéguine.*
> Trans. by Lt.-Col. Spalding.

ALBERT

On the evening of the 27th March, 1821, was presented a new ballet, *Paris et Œnone*, composed for Albert, who made his first appearance at this time. It is not often that a performer establishes his reputation at a theatre to which he is a stranger, by one representation ; but Albert's Paris displayed a buoyant elegance of motion that at once stamped him in public as a first-rate dancer. So great, indeed, was the admiration excited that Mr. John Fuller shouted out from the boxes his satisfaction in the words : " You dance excellently well ! "

John Ebers. *Seven Years of the King's Theatre.*

EMILIA BIGOTTINI AND FANNY BIAS

Such beauty—such grace—oh, ye sylphs of romance !
  Fly, fly to Titania, and ask her if *she* has
One light-footed nymph in her train that can dance
  Like divine Bigottini and sweet Fanny Bias !
Fanny Bias in Flora—dear creature—you'd swear,
  When her delicate feet in the dance twinkle round,
That her steps are of light, that her home is the air,
  And she only *par complaisance* touches the ground.

And when Bigottini in Psyche dishevels
  Her black flowing hair, and by dâemons is driven,
Oh ! who does not envy those rude little devils
  That hold her and hug her and keep her from
    heaven ?

Thomas Moore. *The Fudge Family in Paris.*

MARIE TAGLIONI

Will the young folk ever see anything so charming,
anything so classic, anything like Taglioni?

Thackeray. Pendennis.

MARIE TAGLIONI

Elle était cette fois la sylphide rêvée,
Que, sous le ciel d'Ecosse, un poète a trouvée,
Divinité qui suit les pâtres au sillon,
Aime les laboureurs, visite les chaumières,
Et pendant la veillée, agite les lumières
　　Avec son vol de papillon.

Regardez-la courir !   Rien de mortel en elle.
On craint de la blesser lorsqu'on touche son aile :
Quand elle prend son vol, les regards soucieux
Semblent la retenir au sol qu'elle abandonne.

Méry.

MARIE TAGLIONI

During Marie Taglioni's visit to Russia, there was
published an engraving by Wright after General
Kiel, of her daintily-shod foot raised *sur la pointe*
and surrounded by clouds.   Below the drawing was
a quatrain in Russian by Prince Viazemsky, the sense
of which was again expressed in the single French
phrase :

Pourquoi chausser une aile ?

FANNY ELSSLER

Qui voudrait mettre à prix un talent si charmant,
Trouverait-il au monde un égal diamant ?
Dans trois simples joyaux notre offrande s'exprime :
Reconnaissance, amour, inalterable estime.

Lensky-Moreau.

FANNY ELSSLER

A Fanny Elssler, les artistes de Moscou—
Au cœur le plus noble au talent le plus beau.

[Inscription on a bracelet presented to F. Elssler in 1871 by the artistes
of the Imperial Theatre, Moscow.]

CARLOTTA GRISI

Presenté à Mdlle. Carlotta Grisi, la danseuse la plus poétique de l'univers, avec les hommages respectueux de son directeur A. Bunn, Theatre Royal, Drury-lane. 18th November, 1843.

[Inscription on a bracelet presented to C. Grisi on the occasion of the last performance that season of *La Péri*.]

CARLOTTA GRISI

Ah ! du moins nous avons la Danse, art divin !
Et l'homme le plus fait pour être écrivain. . . .
Ne pourrait découvrir l'ombre d'un iota
Pour défendre à ses vers d'admirer Carlotta.
Son corps souple et nerveux a des suaves lignes ;
Vive comme le vent, douce comme les cygnes,
L'aile d'un jeune oiseau soutient ses pieds charmants,
Ses yeux ont des reflets comme des diamants,
Ses lèvres à l'eden auraient servi de portes.
    Théodore de Banville. *Odes Funambulesques*.

LÉONTINE BEAUGRAND

Qui nous consolera de ton triste départ,
De ton injuste exil, savante enchanteresse,
Dont le pas élégant à sa chaste caresse,
Sans corrompre le cœur, enchaînait le regard ?

Tu forçais les penseurs à respecter ton art,
Car c'est par toi qu'émus d'une noble allégresse
Ils comprenaient pourquoi les Sages de la Grèce
Au culte de la Danse avaient marqué sa part.

C'est par toi, par ton vol aux courbes expressive,
Que des ailes de l'âme et des lignes du corps
Nous sentions les profonds et merveilleux accords.

Si tes grâces, Beaugrand, doivent rester oisives,
Qui nous rendra l'extase où tu nous ravissais
Par ton charme si fin, si pur et si français ?
                    Sully Prudhomme.

LÉONTINE BEAUGRAND IN 1867

She dances no longer, she flies.

Nestor Roqueplan.

ROSITA MAURI

Attiré par le feu, grisé par le rayon,
Le papillon tournoie et se grille à la flamme ;
Mais, lorsque vous dansez, Rosita, c'est notre âme
Qui voltige et se brûle autour du papillon.

François Coppée.

ANNA PAVLOVA

She was first and last a great individual artist, a complete unity in herself, who had the supreme power of not only being able to breathe into a dance her own flame-like spirit, but, no matter how many times she had danced it before, to invest it with an air of spontaneity, novelty, and freshness, as though it had but just been born. She was something more than a great artist-dancer. She made her features speak and her body sing.

C. W. Beaumont. *Anna Pavlova.*

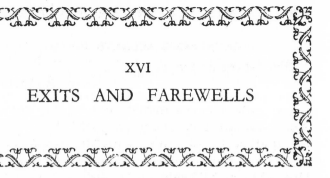

CAMARGO IN RETIREMENT

I had the good fortune, on returning to Paris, to find Camargo still dancing ; but she was in her autumn and even neared her winter.

She has since lived in a peaceful and honourable retirement, with half a dozen dogs, and the one friend who remains to her out of all her thousand and one lovers, to whom she has bequeathed her dogs.

Grimm. *Correspondance Littéraire.*

THE FUNERAL OF MARIE CAMARGO
(Paris, April 29th, 1770)

He [a friend] gave her a magnificent burial, and everyone admired the white hangings, symbol of virginity, which unmarried persons have the right to use in their funeral ceremonies.

Grimm. *Correspondance Littéraire.*

GUIMARD IN RETIREMENT

Despréaux, Mlle. Guimard's husband, entertained his friends by using his fingers to imitate the most celebrated dancers of his time. I believe that the first idea of this toy came about thus: Already married to that former dancer, and living at the Rue de Ménars on the right as you enter the Rue de Richelieu, in the house where there is now an insurance office, Mlle. Guimard continued to receive, as before the Revolution, a numerous and pleasant company. During these intimate conversations the memory of her former triumphs naturally recurred

to all those present, praise followed praise, and
regret was expressed that it was not possible to form
a conception of that wonderful talent to which a
whole generation had been pleased to render homage.
Some indiscreet visitors clamoured for something
which would give them an idea of it. At last,
in deference to this flattering demand, the
septuagenarian dancer arranged (but without
fatiguing herself) some *pas* likely to explain her
former European success. Good-humoured,
obliging, and high-spirited as she was, Mlle.
Guimard erected some light barriers against her
age and the ravages of time which such goodwill
might make too obvious. But her husband, ever
ready to entertain his friends with some mechanical
contrivance instead of his so-called amusing poems,
thought to satisfy her petitioners thus: He built
a stage the length of the room with a drop curtain
so fixed that it permitted only the legs of the dancers
to be seen. Then he and his wife, rigged out only
in those parts that were visible, the bottom of a
spangled tunic and the traditional shoes, presented
those portions of their bodies to the judgment of
the spectators without compromising what youth
yet remained to them by not showing the old age
which the remainder of their persons would have
revealed.

Ah well, many witnesses of this curtailed performance assured me that the revelations of Mlle.
Guimard's talent were most extraordinary. The
foot, singularly coquettish, had retained all its
suppleness and vigour, the slender and well-turned
leg executed the *pas* with almost the firmness of
youth and the correct execution of the whole recalled
the old school

In short, this spectacle was most captivating, for
through the imagination it gave point to the visible
dance and drama to the miming which was not seen.
This success was prodigious and so noised abroad
that every one begged for seats at these private

performances, and we saw the time when the fashions of yesterday were about to take a new lease of life in the radiance of a select audience. But Mlle. Guimard's health did not allow her to continue for more than five or six evenings, which sufficed to prove that consoling truth—beauty ages but grace never grows old.

Charles Maurice. *Epaves.*

LAST APPEARANCE OF MARIE TAGLIONI
(Paris, June, 1844)

Farewell performances which, however, are not always final, have a certain penetrating and melancholic charm ; it is like the perfume of the last rose whose scent one wishes to savour ; it seems that one is going to set that fleeting glory on the road to prosperity by giving her a farewell round of applause. When the curtain falls on the conclusion, one experiences the same sort of sadness which is felt on seeing a post-chaise carry away one's beloved. The first turn of the wheel is over one's heart.

How immense must be the sadness which succeeds all that noise, all that splendour, all that excitement ! To pass from this glowing atmosphere into the chill shadow of retirement—no longer to see gleam at your feet that circle of flame which separates you from the real world and which makes you greater than a queen ; no longer to overhear beyond the pier of the orchestra the dark, plashing waters of the stalls ! It is true that the waters of Lake Como are of a sparkling azure, that the sun's rays gild the marble villa ; Mignon would be happy there, because there the lemons ripen and golden oranges gleam amid the dark foliage. But will all this enable the retired Sylphide to forget her kingdom of gauze and painted cloth ? Will the sun of Italy console her for the loss of the glamour of the theatre ?

Théophile Gautier. *Histoire de l'Art Dramatique en France depuis Vingt-Cinq Ans.*

M

NECESSITY FORCES MARIE TAGLIONI TO TEACH IN HER OLD AGE

It was a sad sight to see her, white-haired, dressed as if she were a housemaid, superintending an English school at Hyde Park in winter, and at Brighton in summer. She gave lessons in deportment to the Court, where, as is well known, the Queen always had a gallery of beauties. The Princess of Wales learned from Marie Taglioni how to make her royal curtsies almost in the same way as Napoleon studied with Talma how to acquire a majestic presence. To see her accompanied by a diminutive old Italian whose coat-tails swept the floor, as he played in a dancing-master's kit, was to see a character who might have stepped from the pages of Hoffmann.

And so she taught the Pavane, the Romanesca, the Gavotte, the Trenitz, and all the figures of the Cotillon. The poor woman's tremulous voice could be heard crying : " *Pliez ! Pliez !* Miss Helena. *Glissez ! Glissez !* Miss Arabella." It was her swan-song, but neither Miss Helena nor Miss Arabella glided with French grace or bent their knees with Italian facility, and that worried Marie Taglioni.

Arsène Houssaye. *Les Confessions.*

THE FUNERAL OF EMMA LIVRY

She bore too great a likeness to a butterfly ; for she, too, burnt her wings in the flame, and, as if they wished to take part in the funeral of a sister, two white butterflies did not cease from circling over the white coffin during its journey from the church to the cemetery. That incident, which, in Greece, would have been regarded as a poetic symbol, was remarked by thousands of people, for an immense crowd accompanied the hearse. On the simple tomb of the young dancer what epitaph should be written, if not that fashioned for an Emma Livry of antiquity by a poet of the Anthology : " O

Earth, weigh gently upon me, I trod so lightly upon thee."

Indeed, in that lively and tender interest of a whole population, the talent, youth, and fatal end of the victim and her long suffering counted for much ; but there was yet another reason ; there was a desire to honour that life which had remained unsullied despite the easy temptations of her profession, that modest virtue which rendered slander silent, that love of her art and of hard work, which desired no other allurements than the Dance itself ; it was desired to show that one respects an artist who respects herself. If anything can soothe a mother's grief, it was that procession, so solemn, so moving, so completely religious in feeling, which followed the mourning carriage in which, seated amid celebrities of the Opéra, were the two Sisters of Charity who had tended the poor girl during her last hours on earth.

Théophile Gautier. *Portraits Contemporains.*

LÉONTINE BEAUGRAND'S PREMATURE LAST APPEARANCE

To dance the last *pas* to unanimous applause while you are still young, in the flower of your strength and talent, when you love your art, which you have developed with all your soul, the art of French dancing ! What anguish is hidden beneath those farewell smiles ! What bitter joy is in those final shouts of applause !

Anon. *La Vie à Paris.*

CATTERINA BERETTA IN OLD AGE

We paid a preliminary visit to the Signora in the Via dei Tre Alberghi. We found her at her meal in a tiny room of the top flat. A leg of chicken in one hand, Signora Beretta, with a stately flourish of the other, waved us towards her sitting-room, where we waited for some time till a ludicrous little figure waddled in. Fat and short, her pyramidal shape was emphasised by a very small head with a meagre blob of hair on top. From the look of her it was unbelievable that she should have been a great star of the Scala. Dry laurel wreaths, an enlarged photo on an easel draped with fringed ribbons, a quantity of smaller photographs showing the Signora in her youth, always rather plump, firmly and correctly planted on her toes, made a pathetic display round a lonely old woman. She was very courteous. It was agreed that I should join the class in two days, the time allowed for her servant, Marcella, to make my tarlatans and bodice. Towards the end of the interview, Signora Beretta got communicative ; she took me round her little sitting-room, showing me her photographs, giving the names of her parts. We parted friends ; she chucked me under the chin. " *A dopo domani, giovanina.*"

Thamar Karsavina. *Theatre Street.*

NIJINSKY IN RETIREMENT

We [Serge Diaghilev and Anton Dolin] entered the hall, our hats were taken and we were shown into the drawing-room. There, sitting in front of us, like a convalescent invalid, was the greatest of all dancers.

His wife greeted us. I was presented to her. Hardly a word was spoken, but somehow in this man's face there was something more expressive than a volume of words. There were the same eyes I had seen in pictures, the same beautiful mouth, the upper lip clean-shaven and dark, hardly a hair on the head at all, white hands that were never still.

This was Nijinsky !

All around the room were portraits. I distinctly remember Sargent's famous painting of the great dancer.

There were various photographs, flowers in the window, lace curtains—it was almost suburban . . . and then, above a desk, a doctor's chart recording the varying temperatures of the invalid.

Diaghilev tried to make him speak. He wouldn't

say one word. He just sat and laughed. I asked him something and he answered : " *Je ne sais pas.*" Four words that expressed the whole tragedy—he didn't know.

Anton Dolin. Divertissement.

LAST APPEARANCE OF ENRICO CECCHETTI
(London, 5th January, 1922)

At the end of the second act, when Cecchetti was taking his call, the curtain was raised and he was presented with many souvenirs of the occasion by his fellow-artistes. At last the curtain was lowered and then a moving scene was enacted. Imagine some hundred dancers grouped in a circle. In the centre stood Cecchetti and opposite him one of the company who read out a long speech in Russian, which set forth his history, his triumphs, the love and honour they bore him as a great artist and kindly teacher, and lastly, their congratulations to him on that night of his jubilee. The old man listened with bent head, then, as the words conjured up vision after vision of dancers ; some passed down the long valley, some too old to dance, some he had known as children and who even then were standing by his side ; his eyes became dimmed and the rough texture of his grease-paint was furrowed by a hot tear. He was embraced, kissed by all, lifted shoulder-high and carried in triumph to his dressing-room.

C. W. Beaumont. Enrico Cecchetti.

MAESTRO CECCHETTI GIVES HIS LAST LESSON

On November 12, 1928, he left his home at 8 o'clock and went to La Scala to give his usual morning lesson, which began at 9 o'clock. At first, all went well ; then some movement displeased him and he cried : " No ! No ! It is not so ! " He protested, scolded, then began to cough violently. His legs trembled and he sank into a chair. He smiled apologetically, gasped and fainted. A doctor was called ; the teacher's sons and brother were hastily summoned.

But as the stricken old man made no movement, he was taken to his home. He never recovered consciousness and expired a little before dawn of the next day.

C. W. Beaumont. *Enrico Cecchetti.*

THE LYING-IN-STATE OF ANNA PAVLOVA

On the following Wednesday [January 28th, 1931] her body was brought to London, to lie in state at the Russian Church of St. Philip, in Buckingham Palace Road, that the many admirers of her art might take a last farewell of the one who had given them so many hours of pure happiness. The setting was simple and unostentatious ; there was nothing to suggest the passing of a world-famous star. In the centre aisle and close by the chancel stood a polished black coffin, raised high on trestles. On each side stood a line of three lighted candles set in tall brass candlesticks. One end of the coffin was draped with a Russian flag, the other end was encircled by a wreath, inscribed in English and Russian : "To the Immortal Pavlova from her Company." Numbers of floral tributes were massed about the bier, and still more wreaths were placed against the chancel steps and rails. Through the dark church, the air misty with the fumes of incense and perfumed with the scent of hyacinths and lilies of the valley, moved in an unending file, the dark figures of the mourners, silhouetted against the shifting candlelight.

C. W. Beaumont. *Anna Pavlova.*

SOME DANCERS WHO MARRIED DANCERS

Gaetano Vestris—Marie Allard (1), Marie Heinel (2).
Auguste Vestris—Anne Catherine Augier.
Pierre Gardel—Mlle. Miller.
Jean Etienne Despréaux—Madeleine Guimard.
Dauberval—Mlle. Théodore.
M. Montessu—Mlle. Paul.
Jules Perrot—Carlotta Grisi.
Arthur Saint-Léon—Fanny Cerrito.
Louis Mérante—Zina Richard.
Marius Petipa—Marie Sergeyevna Surovtchikova.
Enrico Cecchetti—Giuseppina de Maria.
Sergey Leonidovich Grigoriev—Lubov Pavlovna Tchernicheva.
Vaslav Fomich Nijinsky—Romola de Pulszky.
Nicholas Nikolayvich Singaevsky—Bronislava Fominichna Nijinska.
Peter Nikolayvich Vladimorov—Felia Leontievna Dubrovska.

SOME LONG-LIVED DANCERS

Louis Pécourt (1655—1729) 74.
Louis Dupré (1697—1774) 77.
Jean Georges Noverre (1727—1809) 82.
Gaetano Vestris (1729—1808) 79.
Madeleine Guimard (1743—1816) 73.
Pierre Gardel (1758—1840) 82.
Auguste Vestris (1760—1842) 82.
Charles Louis Didelot (1767—1837) 70.
Nicholas Osipovich Goltz (1800—1872) 72.

Marie Taglioni (1804—1884) 80.
Auguste Bournonville (1805—1879) 74.
Fanny Elssler (1810—1884) 74.
Carlotta Grisi (1821—1899) 78.
Lucile Grahn (1821—1907) 86.
Marius Petipa (1822—1910) 88.
Enrico Cecchetti (1850—1928) 78.

SOME SHORT-LIVED DANCERS

Nastasia Parfentievna Birilova (1778—1804) 26.
Marie Danilova (1795—1812) 17.
Nastasia Semenovna Novitskaya (1797—1822) 25.
Emma Livry (1842—1863) 21.
Joseppa Bozacchi (1854—1870) 16.

DANCERS AND THEIR PETS

In the official inventory of the property left by Marie Camargo at her death in 1770 are listed several dogs, six parrots, a number of canaries, and fourteen pair of pigeons.

*

During the eighteen-nineties, when Marie Taglioni conducted a select school of dancing in London, she kept two pets—a parrot and a dog. The latter was a pedigree King Charles called Grisi, possibly after the dancer, Carlotta Grisi.

*

Fanny Elssler retired from the stage in 1851 and four years later made her permanent home in Vienna. There she lived in a delightful house with a veranda peopled with birds.

*

Anna Pavlova was very fond of all animals and a long essay could be written on the various dogs alone which she possessed at different times. Perhaps the most cherished of them all was Poppy, a Boston terrier which was her constant companion for five years, and appears with his mistress in several photographs. At her residence, Ivy House, Golder's Green, Pavlova had two swans, the best known being Jack. In addition she had a large number of birds, mainly acquired during her several tours to the Far East. When Pavlova was at Ivy House, the birds were housed in an enormous cage built in the centre of the green-house at the side of the house.

FOOD NAMED AFTER DANCERS

There are several dishes and sweets to which the name of a dancer has been attached, the most favoured being that of Camargo. The following list, to which are added other dishes and sweets whose titles suggest honour to the Dance, are described in Escoffier's *Guide to Modern Cookery* : *Bombe Camargo* (p. 804), *Filet de Bœuf Camargo* (p. 354), *Ris de Veau grillés Camargo* (p. 411), *Soufflé à la Camargo* (p. 739), *Bombe Coppélia* (p. 804), *Sylph's Omelet* (p. 728), and *Sylphides de Volaille* (p. 529).

*

On the occasion of the fiftieth anniversary of the appearance on the stage of the celebrated Russian dancer, N. O. Goltz, which took place on the 22nd February, 1872, a dinner was given in his honour on the 9th March, which included dishes specially devised for the occasion, such as *Consommé à la Didelot* and *Pouding à la Goltz*.

*

During the performances of *The Sleeping Princess* at the Alhambra Theatre, London, in 1922–3, *Pêche Spessiva* was available in the refreshment room.

*

Comparatively recently the chef of the Savoy Grill, London, devised two dishes in honour of well-known dancers of to-day—*Timbale Nikitina* and *Salade de Volaille Ninette de Valois*.

The former is a sweet made up of chocolate and meringue. The latter is a cold chicken salad, including celery, tomatoes, artichokes, and asparagus-tips. Served with it is a special sauce of tomato juice, oil, vinegar, and mustard.

WHEN WHITE TIGHTS WERE WORN

A Right Reverend Prelate, in his place in the House of Lords, gravely accuses the French Directory of sending over French dancers to corrupt the morals of the English nation. That such an *exhibition* as *Parisot's* may warm the blood of a Bishop we can easily conceive, but we do not think the French Directory were at the bottom of it.

The effect of dancing postures must be very extraordinary, since they make an impression not only upon those who *see* them, but even upon grave Prelates who have the *rebound* at *second-hand*.

*

In consequence of the wish of the Manager [of the Opera House] to conform to the public desire, and of which his promptitude upon this occasion is a striking proof, the ballet of *Bacchus & Ariadne*, was postponed, and that of *Constante & Alcidonis* substituted, till the dresses can be prepared for the former. A printed paper was circulated in the Theatre, acquainting the audience of the change. The motives of it are believed to have originated in the remarks made a few evenings ago in an august Assembly upon the tendency of French manners to corrupt the morals of the people of this country, and the conduct of the Opera Manager in attending to such remarks, is deserving of honourable report. In the *reform* perceptible on Saturday evening among the dancers were white stockings instead of flesh-coloured, and a little more drapery above and below.

Morning Chronicle. 6th March, 1798.

HERO-WORSHIP EXTRAORDINARY

Marie Taglioni left Russia for the last time in March, 1842, and the contents of her house were sold by auction. Among the goods was a pair of ballet-shoes which realised 200 roubles. These shoes were cooked, served with a special sauce, and eaten at a dinner organised by a group of balleto-mancs.

Alexander Pleschayev. *Nash Balet.*

SERGE LIFAR WEARS A BLACK SCARF IN TOKEN OF MOURNING FOR HIS MASTER

The news of Cecchetti's death, which took place on the 12th November, 1928, was received by the Diaghilev Company, then dancing at Manchester, on the 15th. The same evening, when Lifar danced in *Les Sylphides,* he wore a black scarf in token of the company's grief at the passing of their cherished friend and teacher.

C. W. Beaumont. *Enrico Cecchetti.*

THE SECRET OF NIJINSKY'S ABILITY TO REMAIN POISED IN THE AIR

She [Bronislava Nijinsky] was the first to impress upon me the importance of breathing in dancing. I remember her explaining more in movements than in words how to hold my breath while my body was suspended in the air and only when it had descended to the ground to expand gradually. She told me, then, how the secret of this had been largely the cause that governed her brother's jump, and that pause in the air which all who have seen him dance remember so well.

Anton Dolin. *Divertissement.*

BIBLIOGRAPHY

Anon. *Ces Demoiselles de l'Opéra.*

Anon. *La Vie à Paris.*

Arago, Jacques. *Physiologie des Foyers.* Paris. 1841.

Arbeau, Thoinot. *Orchésographie.* Langres. 1589.

Baudelaire, Charles. *Fanfarlo des Paradis Artificiels.* Paris. 1889.

Beaumont, C. W. *Anna Pavlova.* London. 1932.

Beaumont, C. W. *La Boutique Fantasque.* London. 1919.

Beaumont, C. W. *Enrico Cecchetti.* London. 1929.

Beaumont, C. W. *The Three-Cornered Hat.* London. 1919.

Blasis, Carlo. *The Code of Terpsichore.* Trans. R. Barton. London. 1830.

Blessington, Lady. *The Idler in France.* London. 2 Vols. 1841.

Bournonville, Auguste. *Etudes Chorégraphiques.* Copenhagen. 1861.

Bunn, Alfred. *The Stage.* London. 3 Vols. 1840.

Casanova de Seingalt, G. G. *Mémoires.* Paris. 8 Vols. 1880.

Castil-Blaze. *Histoire de l'Académie Impériale de Musique.* Paris. 2 Vols. 1855.

Chesterfield, Lord. *Letters to his Son.* London. 2 Vols. 1774.

Chorley, H. F. *Thirty Years' Musical Recollections.* London. 2 Vols. 1862.

Dandré, Victor. *Anna Pavlova.* London. 1932.

De Balzac, Honoré. *La Paix du Ménage.*

De Banville, Théodore. *Odes Funambulesques.* Paris. 1892.

De Boigne, Charles. *Petits Mémoires de l'Opéra.* Paris. 1857.

De Cahusac. *La Danse Ancienne et Moderne.* The Hague. 1754.

De Créquy, Marquise. *Souvenirs.* Paris. 10 Vols. 1842.

De Ligne, Prince. *Mémoires et Lettres.* Paris. 1923.

Desarbres, Nerée. *Sept Ans à l'Opéra.* Paris. 1864.

Despréaux, J. E. *Mes Passetemps.* Paris. 2 Vols. 1866.

Despréaux, J. E. *Souvenirs.* Issondon. 1894.

Diderot, D. and D'Alembert, J. L. *Encyclopédie.* Geneva. 17 Vols. 1765-72.

D'Oberkirch, Baronne. *Mémoires.* Paris. 1853.

Dolin, Anton. *Divertissement.* London. 1931.

Dorat, C. J. *La Déclamation Théâtrale.* Paris. 1761.

Duthé, C. R. *Souvenirs.* Paris. 1909.

Ebers, John. *Seven Years of the King's Theatre.* London. 1828.

Gautier, Théophile. *Les Beautés de l'Opéra.* Paris. 1845.

Gautier, Théophile. *Histoire de l'Art Dramatique en France depuis Vingt-Cinq Ans.* Paris. 6 Vols. 1858-9.

Gautier, Théophile. *Portraits Contemporains.* Paris. 1874.

Golovacheva-Panaeva, A. Y. *Memoirs.*

Grimm. *Correspondance Littéraire, Philosophique et Critique adressée à un Souverain d'Allemagne.* Paris. 17 Vols. 1812-14.

Gronow, Capt. *Reminiscences and Recollections.* London. 2 Vols. 1889.

Guillemin. *Chorégraphie, ou l'Art d'écrire la Danse.* Paris. 1784.

Hone, Philip. *Diary.* (New York Public Library.)

Houssaye, Arsène. *Les Confessions.* Paris. 1885.

Janin, Jules. *The American in Paris.* London. 1843.

Janin, Jules. *Pictures of the French*. London. 1841.

Jenyns, Soame. *The Art of Dancing*. London. 1729.

Karamzin, N. M. *Voyage en France*. 1789-90. Traduit du Russe par A. Legrelle. Paris. 1885.

Karsavina, Thamar. *Theatre Street*. London. 1930.

Kelly, Michel. *Reminiscences*. London. 2 Vols. 1826.

Lamennais, H. F. R. *De l'Art et du Beau*. Paris. 1885.

Larousse, Pierre. *Grand Dictionnaire Universel du XIXe Siècle*. Paris. 15 Vols. 1866.

Legat, Nicholas. *The Story of the Russian School*. Trans. from the Russian by Sir Paul Dukes. London. 1932.

Lemercier de Neuville, Louis. *Marie Petipa*. Paris. 1861.

Levinson, André. *La Danse au Théâtre*. Paris. 1924.

Levinson, André. *La Danse d'Aujourd'hui*. Paris. 1929.

Locke, John. *Some Thoughts Concerning Education*. London. 1693.

Lucian. *Works*. Trans. by H. W. Fowler and F. G. Fowler. London. 4 Vols. 1905.

Lumley, Benjamin. *Reminiscences of the Opera*. London. 1864.

Maurice, Charles. *Histoire Anecdotique du Théâtre*. Paris. 2 Vols. 1856.

Maurice, Charles. *Épaves*. Paris. 1865.

Métra, François. *Correspondance Secrète*. Neuwied. 18 Vols. 1787-9.

Molière. *Le Bourgeois Gentilhomme*.

Moore, Thomas. *The Fudge Family in Paris*. London. 1817.

Nijinsky, Romola. *Nijinsky*. London. 1933.

Noverre, J. G. *Lettres sur la Danse, les Ballets, et les Arts*. St. Petersburg. 4 Vols. 1803-4.

Oxford English Dictionary. Vol. III (1). Oxford. 1897.

Parfait, François et Claude. *Histoire de l'Académie Royale de Musique*. 1695. (In MS., Bibliothèque Nationale, Paris.)

Petit de Bachaumont, Louis. *Mémoires Secrets*. London. 36 Vols. 1777-89.

Pleshchayev, Alexander. *Nash Balet*. St. Petersburg. 1897.

Pushkin, A. S. *Eugene Onéguine*. Trans. from Russian by Lt.-Col. Spalding. London. 1881.

Rameau, P. *Le Maître à Danser*. Paris. 1725.

Raynaud, Jacques. *Portraits Contemporains*. Paris.

Sala, G. A. *A Journey due North*. London. 1859.

Séchan, Charles. *Souvenirs d'un Homme de Théâtre*. Paris. 1883.

Second, Albéric. *Les Petits Mystères de l'Opéra*. Paris. 1844.

Smith, Albert. *Natural History of the Ballet Girl*. London. 1847.

Stern, Daniel. *Mes Souvenirs*. Paris. 1877.

Thackeray, W. M. *Pendennis*. London. 2 Vols. 1849.

Thackeray, W. M. *Roundabout Papers*. London. 1863.

Valéry, Paul. *Eupalinos, ou l'Architecte* ; precédé de *l'Âme et la Danse*. Paris. 1923.

Véron, Dr. L. *Mémoires d'un Bourgeois de Paris*. Paris. 6 Vols. 1856.

Vigée-Lebrun, Marie. *Souvenirs*. Paris. 2 Vols. 1867.

Vizentini, Albert. *Derrière la Toile*. Paris. 1868.

Voltaire. *Siècle de Louis XIV*. Berlin. 2 Vols. 1751.

Walpole, Horace. *Letters*. Edit. by Mrs. Paget Toynbee. 16 Vols. Oxford. 1903-5.

Weaver, John. *Anatomical and Mechanical Lectures upon Dancing*. London. 1721.

William the Jew, of Pesaro. *De Practica seu arte tripudii.* 1460. (In MS. Bibliothèque Nationale, Paris.)

Willis, N. P. *Famous Persons and Famous Places.* London. 1854.

Yates, G. *The Ball.* London. 1829.

Zorn, F. A. *Grammatik der Tanzkunst.* Leipzig. 1887.

Constitutionnel, Le. 17th November, 1862.

Dancing Times, The. December, 1921.

Dancing World, The. June and December, 1922.

Examiner, The. 6th June, 1830.

Fanfare. December, 1921.

Figaro Illustré, Le. February, 1895.

Illustrated London News, The. 21st December, 1844.

Je Sais Tout. 5th November, 1912.

Journal de l'Empire, Le. 1st and 10th March, 1807.

Journal des Débats, Le. 15th December, 1845.

Journal de Paris. 7th May, 1820.

Mercure de France. January and September, 1732 ; July, 1756.

Monthly Chronicle, The. July–December, 1838.

Morning Chronicle, The. 24th February, 1781 ; 6th March, 1798.

Morning Herald, The. 6th March, 1788; April, 1789.

Programme of His Majesty's Theatre. 23rd February, 1847.

Spectator, The. 17th May, 1711.

Tatler, The. 1st November, 1709.

University Magazine, The. April, 1789.